The Quest for Intimacy

Nathan R. Grooms M.A.

"This book is the overflow of the author's five decades of counseling and teaching on the topic of marital intimacy. It is extremely practical and includes many real-life examples. It points the way for Christians to experience spiritual, emotional, and sexual intimacy. I highly recommend it for any couple who would like to have a growing intimacy in their relationship."

Gary Chapman, Ph.D. author of

The Five Love Languages.

"I have worked on a church staff with Nathan for more than 30 years. I don't know of anyone who has more passion, compassion, and love for ministry to married couples than he does. He has counseled with more couples than I could possibly count and God has used him to bring countless victories in marriages that were facing deep challenges.

He is a man after God's own heart and serves as the greatest example of anyone I know of how to love the way our Father loves. You will enjoy reading this book and you will learn to be a better husband or wife in the process."

Mike Divine

Senior Pastor

at Covenant Church Lincolnton, NC.

Dedication

To Suzette (Suzy), my Christ-honoring, beach-loving wife of almost 43 years, who deeply loved her family and family time. Prior to her passing, she shared all the experiences of young love and maturing love with me. She was my best friend and constant supporter.

To my children Aaron, Amber, and Andrew, who prayerfully learned the joys and benefits of a Christ-centered marriage through their parents' sincere effort to apply such truths as unconditional love, forgiveness, grace, patience, and much more with each other. May the embarrassing hugs and kisses you witnessed growing up always serve as a reminder to you now in your married life that your spouse also needs and deserves constant expressions of love and affection.

Aaron's wife Lori, sons Davis and Luke; Amber's husband Marty, children Rachel and Blake; Andrew's wife Amber; and children Hudson and Harrison, who all have brought unlimited amounts of love, joy, happiness, and wisdom into our family. May the love of God rule and reign in your hearts and families for generations to come.

Also, to Vickie (Vic), my wife in this latter season of life, who so deeply understands my heart and calling to strengthen marriages and share the life-changing truths of the gospel. Thank you, Vic, for your love that both embraces and encourages me and loves my entire family as no one else could. May our "Road Trips" continue for many more miles.

Some individuals go through life and never feel as though they have known true love once. I have been blessed to experience true love twice, and the fact that they both have loved riding in a convertible without worrying about their hair has been a tremendous bonus to this man.

I am blessed indeed!

Nathan

Acknowledgments

My heartfelt appreciation to Dr. Gary Chapman who has been a wonderful friend and mentor for over 17 years. I am extremely grateful for all that he has shared with me about both writing and life in general. His influence serves as a constant reminder to be faithful to the calling and to seek the Lord's guidance in every decision.

To Kim Pittman, whose untold hours of editing, expertise, and encouragement have helped make this book a reality. As this project grew, Kim's determination and faithfulness grew along with it to see it through.

To the faithful members of our Love's Journey leadership group, as well as many within the class and those who have attended seminars where I was teaching, for your encouragement to share more insight and inspiration in a written format.

Your encouragement has been deeply appreciated

Table of Contents

Introduction 1

Part I ~ The Value of Spiritual Intimacy 5

   Chapter 1: *Your New Beginning* 6

   Chapter 2: *The Importance of a Spiritual Foundation* .. 19

   Chapter 3: *Steps to Spiritual Intimacy for Couples* 34

   Chapter 4: *Steps to Spiritual Intimacy - Praying Together Out Loud* 39

   Chapter 5: *Steps to Spiritual Intimacy – Worshiping* 50

   Chapter 6: *Steps to Spiritual Intimacy – Becoming One through Inspirational Truths* 62

   Chapter 7: *Steps to Spiritual Intimacy* 82

Part II ~ The Importance of Emotional Intimacy 96

   Chapter 8: *Searching For Personal Oneness* 97

   Chapter 9: *Understanding Emotional Intimacy* 106

   Chapter 10: *The Gift of Each Other* 136

   Chapter 11: *Embracing Your Future* 148

   Chapter 12: *Defining Emotional Intimacy* 164

Part III ~ The Gift of Physical and Sexual Intimacy 172

   Chapter 13: *Free To Love* 173

   Chapter 14: *Hindrances To Intimacy* 189

   Chapter 15: *We Are Created So Differently* 207

   Chapter 16: *Becoming The Lover, You Want And Need* 227

Introduction

Since the beginning of time, every person has been created for relationships. You are no exception. There is a yearning in every heart to experience and enjoy deep and fulfilling relationships. We could all agree that no couple ever walked down the aisle to get married hoping for a shallow relationship that would leave them feeling frustrated and with unfulfilled dreams.

This book's purpose is to help married couples or individuals who one day hope to be married, understand more about the truth and depth of intimacy. As you read through these pages, you will learn that intimacy is far more than an occasional heartfelt conversation or a single night of physical passion.

Without question, some couples have many similar interests and dreams that allow them to share and enjoy life together. This creates a measure of happiness and a certain level of fulfillment. For this couple, life is good, though not always perfect.

We must also acknowledge that it is not unusual for opposites to attract in relationships. Initially, one may feel young and alive due to the spontaneity and lightheartedness of their partner. It may also be that the one who is so spontaneous appreciates the organization and structure of their partner.

However, later in life, a deep resentment may develop as one begins to see their spouse as out-of-control and irresponsible while the other ends up feeling as though their love interest has become dull or even controlling.

Introverts fall in love with extroverts. Savers fall in love with spenders. Communicators fall in love with those who prefer single-word answers and head nods. Therefore, we find ourselves in the quest for intimacy. Loving and fulfilling relationships don't just happen. They are the result of understanding, compassion, forgiveness, and trust.

These truths, as well as others that we will learn about throughout this book, have motivated me to understand and pursue the truth about intimacy and the depth of oneness and love.

Please consider the very definition of the words 'quest' and 'intimacy'.

Quest: a search or pursuit made in order to find or obtain something. A predetermined journey to obtain something or arrive at a desired location.

I believe that the word "quest" summarizes the journey for intimacy. Obtaining true, deep, life-changing intimacy requires an ongoing effort that can become challenging, and for some, exhausting. There are times in this journey when a husband or wife may have to take a deep breath, much as you would if you were hiking. Sometimes one partner may even feel like they are climbing a steep hill while their companion is dragging along behind them at a different pace, grasping onto their backpack and pulling them backward just to stay together. In some situations, one or both partners are simply trying to stay committed for the remaining years of the marriage. Either out of concern or despair, one sometimes looks at their spouse and sternly says, "Let go of me; I'm tired of you holding me back. I would have thought that you would have supported and helped me succeed in life." The firm grip they feel pulling them back could be spiritual, emotional, physical, or even a combination of these things. Is their spouse simply having a bad attitude or not caring? It's usually not that cut and dry.

For years, I have taught a couple's class that I named "Love's Journey". As I envisioned this new class and the following teachings, I could clearly see that every married couple is on a personal journey. After years of marriage, many couples make the mistake of placing their relationship on cruise control. That would be no more effective than putting your car on cruise control and leaving it there. There are curves and dips in the road as well as hills to climb and descend, not to mention the other vehicles (or individuals) that we will need to maneuver around during our marital journey. When driving, we are always required to pay attention to our surroundings and not become distracted. I see that same scenario within marriage. We must be aware of our surroundings and not allow ourselves to become distracted from the responsibility we have of truly getting to know our spouse as well as to love and fulfill them deeply.

Now let's consider the definition of intimacy.

Intimacy -a closeness and vulnerability two individuals share that develops from a loving and trusting relationship. The deepest levels of intimacy include spiritual, emotional and physical oneness.

A Great definition of intimacy that has been shared before is:

"In-To- Me- See"

True intimacy allows us to develop a trusting and vulnerable relationship so that we can honestly open our hearts to our husbands and wives as they do the same toward us. This openness and oneness create an atmosphere of loving trust that leads to the deepest levels of intimacy and oneness.

So please join us and the countless other couples who are in "The Quest for Intimacy."

Part I ~ The Value of Spiritual Intimacy

Chapter 1: *Your New Beginning*

Your new beginning could be right around the corner.

Some time ago when I announced to a large group of couples that I was going to teach them about intimacy, several of the men began smiling ear to ear. A couple of them even did a fist bump in the air, believing that I was about to teach a lesson that would encourage their wives to be more responsive to their sexual advances and desires.

There were even some awkward giggles in the room, as well as numerous expressions that demonstrated everyone in the room was interested in the following lesson for various reasons. Much to their surprise, especially to many of the men, I announced that the teaching was going to begin on the importance of "spiritual intimacy" within a relationship. It may not have sounded as exciting initially to everyone, but in my opinion, the couple who truly understands and experiences a deep and ongoing spiritual intimacy has a far better chance of mastering and enjoying a deeply fulfilling emotional and physical relationship.

Let's face it, many couples have never seen the need for a spiritual foundation for their marriage. They assume that their initial and often exhilarating feelings of love will carry them throughout their entire marriage. The time will come, however, when the feelings of love will be replaced with the pressures of life's realities. Every area of this couple's marriage will be challenged.

Glenn and Marie's story offers a valuable example. They sat in front of my desk, squirmed nervously, and then began sharing their story with me about the first 15 years of their marriage. It was evident to me that the foundation of their marriage was inadequate. I asked them how they met and about the early days of their relationship. "Sex, sex, sex" was their response. They told me that sex was the basis of their relationship from the very beginning and had been for many years. Both of them were hard-working individuals who excelled in their careers. This allowed them to plan for exotic vacations, which meant a new adventure and, in all honesty, enjoying sex in beautiful new destinations. They were also a popular couple, and there were always other couples over at their house when they were grilling out or playing games. On the outside, it appeared they were living the dream life.

However, they would often quarrel or disagree. Glenn often felt belittled and shamed, while Marie felt rejected and unappreciated. Their one means of resolving the conflicts was more sex which seemed great for the moment but didn't change their attitudes or the deeper issues that were never addressed.

Their limited understanding and expressions of love had left them brokenhearted, empty, and angry with tears rolling down both of their faces. But isn't sex the greatest expression of love? When a couple shares themselves in sexual intimacy, shouldn't it erase the anger and problems they have? Isn't that the greatest way to show your love and commitment to one another and that you care for them? Of course, it is a wonderful expression of love and oneness. That is why the gift is so special and should be shared exclusively with your husband or wife. That one person you have committed your entire life to... forever.

However, sometimes it may be a greater expression of love to refrain from sexual intimacy. Most people fail to understand that sexual intimacy is designed to bond the hearts, minds, and bodies of two individuals together. Not just two bodies.

Suppose sexual intimacy is the greatest expression of love and intimacy. How is it possible that it may lead one couple or individual to feel loved and desired as never before, and yet, in other scenarios, it can make them feel used or even dirty? We will examine physical relationships later in the book.

Being able to live with deep peace and contentment with someone else always begins with you as an individual having peace and contentment within your own heart. Be honest for a moment; does that describe you and your heart? Thousands of friends on social media, professional advancements in your career, and even a huge bank account cannot provide the peace and contentment that is needed in your heart to live in true peace.

Unfortunately, Glenn and Marie learned this truth the hard way. They eventually wondered if they had even made the correct decision when they married one another. They spent years developing their careers and raising their family, just as other couples have done, yet eventually issues surfaced that crushed both of them.

We did not ask to come into this imperfect world as an imperfect individuals. However, that's exactly what happened. We desperately need the Lord's insight and guidance to understand His purpose and plan for our lives. Unless you believe that the Lord has created us and established the true meaning of love and relationships, you will tend to determine and justify your own definitions and standards.

I would suggest to you that you can be sincere and yet be sincerely wrong.

Proverbs 14:12 tells us, "There is a way that appears to be right, but in the end, it leads to death." The reality is that the Lord himself established the required standard for truth and accepted norms before any of us were born. Our hearts and our society are in chaos because we have either intentionally or unintentionally rejected God's norms, standards, and guidelines. Too often we choose to walk within our own self-serving set of guidelines and rules as we go through our daily schedule.

It is imperative that we slow down from our busy pace of life, humble our hearts, and learn and understand His guidelines and commandments for life. Ultimately, we will all be judged by His Word. It would be foolish to live throughout our entire lives and not understand His purpose and will concerning relationships.

So often we are convinced that there are issues in the hearts of our husbands or wives that are causing us constant heartache when the truth is, we don't even know our own hearts. Not really.

Robert and Terri's marriage is a great illustration of this truth. Their marriage greatly improved as did their overall attitudes toward others when they realized that most of their arguments were about trying to get what they wanted or prove a point. How many countless times in your marriage or relationship have you had an argument where you were utterly determined to prove that you were right? Sometimes, you crushed your spouse's heart while doing so or at least destroyed the atmosphere and enjoyment of the day.

Before I begin to share any part of Robert and Terri's story with you, I need to share a portion of my own story and make a confession to you while doing so. One of my life's greatest ambitions has been to be a good husband and father. That being said, I have often failed. I assume that I entered my marriage with two things you can relate to: my realistic marital and unrealistic expectations. When we are young and in love, we think we will meet all of each other's needs and thus live happily ever after. We all know that is not even remotely true. Not in real life.

Today, I honestly do not remember what started this disagreement with my wife Suzy all those years ago, we had been married for several years. Since we had married so young, we were still in our early 20s but old enough to know better. Similarly, many couples have told me that when they look back at days of uncontrollable arguing and displays of disrespect towards one another after the dust had settled, emotions had subsided, and cooler heads prevailed, they honestly could not remember what started their argument.

Whatever the source of the disagreement was, it certainly escalated. We both dug our heels in the sand, believing that we were justified in our requests and attitudes. She probably felt as though I was not being understanding and considerate of her feelings or desires. Most likely, I was feeling disrespected or unappreciated. We both said things that we later wished we had not said, but on that particular day, I was absolutely determined to get in the last word. And I did! As we raised our voices, I made sure that mine was the loudest. When our facial expressions were filled with anger or hurt, I made sure that mine exceeded hers. At the height of our verbal exchange, she began crying. My wife stood there in front of me, and eventually, she was sobbing uncontrollably. My first thought was that after all she had said, and how she made me feel, *it served her right*. However, very quickly, I looked into my wife's eyes, the love of my life, and I saw deep into her broken heart and soul. I felt horrible that I had upset her that much and broken her heart. Honestly, I was still hurt and upset myself, and it took me a little time to process all of that. After all, I wasn't happy either, but it didn't take me any time at all to process the fact that I had missed the mark.

What kind of a man is going to stand there and get loud and intimidating towards his wife? As I stood there wanting to console her and watching her cry I thought, *I would never allow any man to talk to my wife in such a way as to break her heart and crush her spirit like this.* But another man did not do it. I had done it. I asked her repeatedly to forgive me and I quickly asked the Lord to forgive me and teach me how to work through our differences and conflicts in a healthy and Godly way. We discussed the argument we had later that night but without any true resolve. Honestly, emotions were still raw and her heart was still broken. Suzy especially needed some quiet time to think and pray that night. In retrospect, I did as well, but I already had my mind made up that I would live my life differently from that day forward. The next day, I was able to hold her, look into her eyes, and make a promise. I promised her that I would never allow that to happen again as long as we were married, and it never happened again in the wonderful decades of marriage we shared before the Lord called her home.

Even in moments of failure and selfishness, the principles of God's word instruct us how to become more loving individuals. If you are still determined to get in the last word, the loudest word, or the most demeaning word when you and your spouse argue, you are setting yourself up for untold heartache and pain in your future. It's simply not worth it. A self-serving attitude will always push your loved one away and create the opposite environment and display of affection that you both want and need in your heart.

I don't know, maybe I was looking for validation that day, just like Robert. Let's get back to Robert and Terri's story.

Robert finally saw that most of the time, when their arguments happened, he was in reality looking for validation. Most men would not think that is what was happening; instead, they would often think that they were just being a man or "telling it like it is."

Robert also learned something about himself. Even though he had pushed down the hurtful and demeaning memories from the past caused by his dad, the effects of those memories were still there. All of these years later, they were still influencing some of his thoughts and actions. It was true; the degrading attitude of his dad as he was growing up had created a deep wound in his heart that he had never dealt with or admitted was there. Even at age 42, he still had a pocket of anger deeply embedded in his heart. It didn't take much to push that button and create an outburst. Terri was completely exhausted from trying to help her marriage succeed and hold it together for the sake of the children. She had been fussed at, cursed at, and belittled for the last time. She loved Robert and did her best to be a good wife and mom. She had grown up in a loving home where no one raised their voice to anyone else. In her family, they would talk things out even after intense disagreements. Terri often thought of how her family worked through their differences respectfully and lovingly. Now she wondered, *what have I gotten myself into? Will this never end or change?* She had even spoken with her mother about leaving Robert on more than one occasion. She had never believed this was the right thing for a wife to do, but she was desperate, discouraged, and humiliated.

Finally, her prayers were answered. A life-changing experience took place in Robert's heart that must also take place in your heart for you to know and understand the deepest levels of love and intimacy, as well as your purpose in life. He began to see things for what they truly were rather than the way he had always thought they were. Truthfully, at times, he would have bet his last dollar that he was right concerning some of their disagreements.

But he was wrong! Is it possible that you could also be seeing some things inaccurately that are hindering your relationship from flourishing? Don't give up! Wonderful changes may be right around the corner for you just as they were for Robert and Terri.

One day, while at work, one of the men in Robert's department, whom he most admired, came over to him in the cafeteria and asked him if he could speak to him for a moment. Robert had seen Ted as a "man's man" through the years of working together. Ted was known for his adventurous spirit and many outdoor conquests. Everyone knew him as a strong and determined individual, and it did not seem as though anything could stop him from reaching his goals, corporately or otherwise. Since he had seen Ted for years as a man of strength, the last thing he expected during this private conversation was for this bigger-than-life, physically fit man to talk to him with a humble attitude about his private life. Honestly, at first, the conversation even seemed a little awkward.

Ted had gone through a personal transformation in his life. He had also observed the frustration and anger deep in Robert's heart at times, and he was man enough to talk to him about it.

The conversation was a little awkward for Robert in the beginning but not for Ted. Ted felt like he had just climbed the peak of one of the highest mountains anywhere to be found. He was on top of the world. Ted was now enjoying freedom in his life and a peace in his heart he had never known was possible. Ted had gone on a primitive camping trip with a group of men who had hiked miles into the woods and spent a few days backpacking and trout fishing. Around the campfire, a couple of the men began to talk about how their lives had been changed and how much better their marriages had become. They both commented about how they had stopped arguing so much with their wives and made comments about how much better things were since they learned to agree on issues like how to spend their money and raise their children. The weekend marriage seminar they had both attended had become life-changing. And yes, during the guy talk, one of them even mentioned that he and his wife were having sex more often and they both seemed to be enjoying it more. Now Ted had Robert's complete attention.

Somehow, within the 10 minutes of that short conversation, Ted was able to help Robert understand that the best way to get rid of that anger was to pray and turn it over to Christ. He reminded him that Christ in his infinite wisdom already understood where the anger originated in his heart and how to deal with it in a healthy manner.

Robert also began to understand the importance of forgiving his wife even though so many things she was doing and saying were hurting him and making him feel unimportant and rejected. He finally admitted that he was also doing things that were hurting her. Now he was starting to understand how Christ forgave him each day for the things he did wrong and that he should also have that same forgiving attitude towards his wife.

Around that campfire, Ted had learned that every man and woman needs to surrender their life to Christ. When Robert saw a man like Ted share about things in his heart and life that most men don't share about, it genuinely moved him.

The following day after work and after thinking about the things that Ted had shared with him, Robert went out to his workshop where it was quiet and he could think. He did something he had never dreamed he would do; he began to talk to God. He didn't even think about the fact that he was praying to God, but he was sick and tired of being angry and constantly butting heads with his wife, and both of them were upset. He was finished with the arguing, and quite frankly, he was finished with his ongoing personal conflict. He was so tired of being an angry, hurt, and argumentative person. That day his heart was changed. That day his life was changed. That day his marriage was changed. Robert did not know how to pray the prayer that sounded like his pastor's or even Ted's. But that day, as he leaned against the workbench in his shop, he asked Christ to forgive him for acting the way that he had towards his wife and others and to come into his heart and change him forever. Often it was the roar of the engine of Robert's sports car coming out of that garage, but on this particular day, it was a prayer of regret and repentance that turned into gratefulness and hope that was ringing through the air.

This life-changing experience deeply touched Robert and it took him a while to collect himself, but once he did, he almost ran into the house to share the good news with Terri. Even though this was exactly what she had been praying for, she could hardly believe it herself. As tears of happiness rolled down her cheeks she hugged Robert and said, "I just know things will work out now. I am so proud of you."

After that, Robert and Terri decided that they would try to have conversations with one another without arguing. Honestly, it was challenging, and they both had to work hard at it because they still tended to want to criticize each other so often. But as they began to spend more time sharing their true feelings and desires, having those conversations got easier. As the critical remarks were seldom being made anymore, they both found themselves feeling more relaxed and it became easier to trust one another. They were both pleasantly surprised when they realized how often they found themselves in each other's arms or looking around only to find the other one helping with the children or doing a project around the house without having to be asked.

Yes, your new beginning could be just around the corner.

Chapter 2: *The Importance of a Spiritual Foundation*

We desperately need a spiritual foundation for our marriage, even if we do not realize it.

There is no better place to start learning about marriage and intimacy than from the One who created it. I assure you that the insight and direction you need for establishing a deeply fulfilling and loving relationship will not be found within the cover of a popular men's or ladies' magazine or from Hollywood's latest creation and twist of what a relationship should look like on the big screen.

If someone could honestly say, "I wrote the book which includes every single volume on relationships," wouldn't that get your attention? What if the book included teachings on the following topics:

1. Keys to communicating with the spouse who views almost every situation in life differently from me.
2. How to resolve conflicts with a partner who seems determined to argue and ridicule me.
3. The financial guide to unity and prosperity.
4. Romance and sexual fulfillment.

Wouldn't you read it? Of course, you would! Most people are surprised to learn that this guide to fulfilling and loving relationships was written many years ago. It's called the Bible. Yes, that big book sitting on many bookshelves, often perceived as boring and irrelevant, is truly the inspirational love manual of the ages.

Genesis 1:26-28 sets the stage, "Then God said, "Let Us make man in Our image, according to Our likeness; let them have dominion over the fish of the sea, over the birds of the air, and over the cattle, over all the earth and over every creeping thing that creeps on the earth." So God created man in His own image; in the image of God He created him; male and female He created them. Then God blessed them, and God said to them, "Be fruitful and multiply; fill the earth and subdue it; have dominion over the fish of the sea, over the birds of the air, and over every living thing that moves on the earth." We all need to understand these facts:

1. God created all of humanity.
2. All of humanity was created in His image.
3. He created humanity as both male and female.
4. All of humanity was created to be fruitful and multiply as well as walk in dominion and authority.

Genesis 2:7 tells us that God Himself breathed into the nostrils of man the breath of life and he became a living being.

However, even following the extraordinary creative manifestations of many living creatures by God himself, Scripture says there was still not a helper (partner) comparable to or suitable for Adam. (Genesis 2:20)

At this time a decision was made that would establish God's order for a man's life and all of humanity. Genesis 2:18 says, "And the Lord God said, it is not good that man should be alone, I will make him a helper, one comparable to him."

Interestingly, Scripture reveals that while in a deep sleep, God took one of Adam's ribs and created a woman to partner with him in life. What a beautiful illustration of the heart of God concerning a relationship. God took something that was very close to Adam's heart to create his partner. The material for her creation was not taken from a portion of Adam's body where a woman should feel like she is constantly superior and should be able to control or manipulate her husband, nor was material taken from a portion of his body, such as his foot, where any man would feel like he had the right to walk on or trample his wife's gentle spirit or dreams.

The more you understand God's plan for relationships, the more you will understand it is about the heart. Yes, His heart and will, but also your heart and will as well as your spouse's heart and will.

With Eve's creation, Adam makes the following declaration in Genesis 2:23, "She is now bone of my bones and flesh of my flesh; she shall be called woman because she was taken out of man."

Please note the author of Genesis' immediate instruction, "Therefore, a man shall leave his father and mother and be joined to his wife, and they shall become one flesh. And they were both naked, the man and his wife, and were not ashamed." (Genesis 2:24-25)

Imagine the scene following the Genesis creation! There were stunning heavens with unlimited galaxies, beautiful tender green grass, colorful, fragrant flowers and plants, succulent fruits and vegetables, breathtaking mountains, countless exotic animals, and indescribable life within the beautiful blue waters. And yet, there is still one "need" that is mentioned.

The need a man has for companionship.

Undoubtedly, from God's perspective, this must be an incredibly important need to fill. A few of the most important reasons for this:

1. God's perfect will and plan would be manifested on earth through both men and women.
2. That the heart of man would be fulfilled, inspired, and comforted by his wife as God used him to fulfill His plan.
3. The Godly manifestation of love that the husband would be responsible for sharing with

his wife would also inspire her to flourish in her giftings and purpose as well.

1. Their love for each other would create a desire for emotional and sexual pleasure between them. As children would be born their parents were directed to teach God's word to them so that they would represent His word and heart to their generation.

Without question, according to Scripture, the beginning of God's order for not only the home but also for all of society originated with a God-honoring marriage.

Let's look back at the terminology that the Lord used concerning humanity and marriage.

- ✓ Be blessed
- ✓ Be fruitful
- ✓ Multiply
- ✓ Fill the earth
- ✓ Subdue the earth
- ✓ Walk in dominion authority

Not one word that the Lord speaks about relationship and marriage projects failure, defeat, or the inability to rise above the circumstances and situations within a relationship. So, what's the problem? Why do we have troubles in our relationships if it's supposed to be so wonderful?

The problem or the issue we deal with originated in and is the result of the eventual rebellion and disobedience of Adam and Eve in the Garden of Eden. We can become upset and disappointed with their decisions; however, we are all cut from the same cloth, and unfortunately, we would have done the same thing.

We have no idea how long they were in the garden before this decision was made, but prior to their disobedience, they enjoyed a relationship of innocence, trust, and fulfillment. There were never any critical remarks, offenses leading to rejection, self-centered actions, or demeaning attitudes, and neither one of them ever felt misunderstood, lonely, or self-conscious.

It is the rippling effects of sin or disobedience to God's word in our lives or the life of the one we are in a relationship with that so often leads to hearts being crushed and rejected.

Much could be written about the effects on relationships due to man's disobedience in the garden, but at this time I will only make a few observations.

- Adam and Eve hid from God as they experienced both shame and fear for the first time in their lives.
- Eve was deceived by the most cunning personality in their lives.
- Adam was not deceived. He chose to follow Eve's suggestion and disobey God.

There is a much deeper truth in Adam and Eve's act of hiding than most people realize. Yes, they realized they were naked, and for the first time, they felt the need to be covered up. <u>But far beyond that, they became spiritually and emotionally naked and began hiding their true heart from God and one another.</u>

Instead of walking responsibly through life, both the husband and wife fell victim to one of the effects of sin, and they began to skillfully play, "the blame game." Eve tried to justify herself before God and said, "The serpent deceived me so I ate the fruit." However, the most used one-liner of all time began here with Adam and continues to this day. When God questioned Adam and asked him how he knew he was naked and that he had eaten from the tree Adam said, "The woman that <u>you</u> gave to me, she gave me of this tree and I ate it." (Gen.3:12)

Adam tried to blame both God and Eve. Anybody and everybody except himself. This famous one-liner by Adam is still used in countless ways, there are just different versions of it. Husbands often make comments such as, "If you would just quit running your mouth so much, I wouldn't react like this," or "I wouldn't be dealing with an addiction if it wasn't for your attitude."

Can wives have a tremendous influence on men's actions and attitudes? By all means, they can. Truly, wives have far more impact on the way their husbands think and feel than most wives realize. But the point here is as men, we are responsible for our actions and attitudes regardless of our wife's behavior. And yes, wives are responsible for their actions and attitudes regardless of their husband's behavior. God's design for a relationship is that we would build up one another and complement each other instead of tearing down and ridiculing one another. The decision to do what is right, regardless of another person's actions, shows evidence of both maturity and integrity, as well as your personal willingness to obey God's word. So, if you continue manifesting a demeaning and critical attitude toward your spouse it is evident that there is a lack of maturity and integrity in your life. Stop blaming your spouse and honestly look inside your own heart.

I think the story of Wayne and Gail summarizes this behavior very well.

Fourteen years into their marriage, two children (ages 10 and 7), three different career changes, growing credit card debt, and beginning all over again establishing their family in two different cities with new churches, new schools, etc., and the story was still the same.

It is <u>your</u> fault.

When the two of them were dating and in the early years of marriage, Gail enjoyed such contentment and peace in her heart that she not only would think to herself about how fortunate a young lady she was, but she would often tell her friends and family members about Wayne's wonderful qualities and attitude.

Now, those memories were shattered as she found herself living with a man who often had a quick temper and was not only rude but even had an increasing number of violent outbursts. The memories were quickly fading when she had looked forward to him arriving home after work and walking through the door with a smile and a hug for her and the children. That simple act made her feel so appreciated and safe, it made her feel so loved.

Now, it seemed as though each day, there would almost always be a frustrated and discouraged man walking through the door who would only play with the children for a few minutes before he would start correcting them and rarely acted as though he looked forward to spending time with Gail. What had happened? Gail was so tired of crying and feeling rejected. She honestly felt like she must be Wayne's enemy at times. Oh, they had some days or moments that were enjoyable, but there was an undercurrent that was undeniable and only getting worse. Gail had tried to think through things that had been said and done by either one of them that had brought about this depth of tension and unhappiness. She had cried repeatedly and had also gotten angry and even found herself screaming when no one else was around. She had confided in her best friend and had even spoken in confidence with one of the ladies who helped lead the women's ministry at church. She couldn't understand why she was feeling and acting the way that she had been, this just simply wasn't who she was. Sometimes she would even think to herself, *I have heard of other ladies acting or feeling like this but never dreamed it could possibly be me. Not me. Not us.* After all of her efforts, things were no better and frankly seemed to be getting worse.

Finally, in desperation, Gail decided that she must find the time that the two of them could talk without interruption and discuss their true issues. Gail was wise by choosing a time and place where Wayne would be less distracted and wouldn't be so frustrated. So with her carefully thought out plan, she approached Wayne and said, "Let's talk. I can't stand this any longer." The anger, the frustration, all of the accusations, and the hurt feelings were overwhelming. "How many days have we argued and fussed in front of the children instead of having fun as a family the way we used to? We are not going to argue in front of the children anymore! We are going to start working this out today!"

Hearing this, Wayne assumed what would happen. Gail, who always wanted to talk things out quickly, would eventually go on a rampage and corner him during the conversation she was trying to initiate. With the anger that had built up inside of him, he often felt like Gail was getting in his face or making him feel like he was being pushed into a corner. He didn't realize her true intention; she was pleading for an answer that could bring happiness back to their hearts and home. Unfortunately, it is not unusual when emotions are running high that couples respond in a manner that comes across as very intimidating or negative. Communication is not simply about what you are saying but also about what the other person is hearing and understanding of what you are saying.

Once confronted, Wayne shut down and said, "I don't want to talk about it." As she insisted, he repeated to her that he did not want to talk about it, and then, to her surprise, he expressed that it wouldn't change things anyway. "What do you mean 'it won't change anything'?" she replied. "Exactly what I said!" Wayne sternly repeated. "This conversation won't change anything!" Gail was persistent, "Why do you say that?" Wayne's reply knocked the wind out of her sail, "Because you will never change, and I'm fed up with your sweet smile but belittling attitude! You know, Gail, I'm not in junior high school. I am a grown man and I'm tired of being treated like I'm not."

Gail felt as though she could hardly breathe as she stood there in disbelief. She had asked for an answer, but this was certainly not what she had expected to hear. The truth is that a husband or wife may need to hear the thoughts and feelings of their spouse numerous times before healing and unity can return. It's important to recognize that it may take time to process information that is shared. If you are someone who normally needs time to process, make sure you are conveying this to your spouse. Let them know you care and are trying to work through things, because if you don't, they may feel you aren't trying or don't care.

Wayne and Gail now had their work cut out for them. They were finally getting to the root of some of their true issues and problems. They promised each other that they would begin to discuss their feelings and disappointments with one another regularly but with a new foundation to the conversation. A foundation of "mutual respect." In my opinion, this is one of the most important aspects of not only healthy conversations but also our attitude in general towards our spouse. Having mutual respect towards one another makes a clear statement; neither the husband nor the wife will ever see themselves as more or less important and deserving than their spouse.

> What surprising or revealing comments or observations would your husband or wife possibly share with you if they were confident that they could share them without retaliation or expressions of anger from you?

Most of us enjoy living within our comfort zone and want to avoid all of the confrontation and conflict possible. However, conflict, when handled properly and respectfully, can lead to growth in a relationship that results in deeper levels of contentment, love, and understanding. Trust also grows out of ongoing, honest, and revealing conversations. The deeper we know and understand our spouse, the easier it becomes to open up and become vulnerable to them. How high and how thick are the walls around your heart today? Are you protecting yourself from additional hurt from your spouse's comments, actions, or attitudes? Do previous relationships continue to convey an undercurrent of memories causing you to feel used, rejected, unworthy, or unattractive? Many individuals build these walls without even realizing they have built them. Some not only acknowledge they have built them but may even be at a place in their relationship where they are glad they have built walls, and that they have built them well.

Marriage is about two hearts being shared with one another at the deepest levels. Yes, it is very challenging for many to obtain that deep level of intimacy when they have become disconnected from one another for various reasons. However, it is without question possible to do, and I believe that is the call on our hearts from our Creator. Becoming one in your marriage without losing your individuality is the call from God on our lives. Clearly, both the husband and wife should bring their strengths and gifts to the marriage to help fulfill, complement, and strengthen their spouse.

Your differences are not designed to cause arguments and division.

There will be many who read this who already know that they must stop looking at their husband or wife through critical, demeaning eyes of frustration and anger. They know they should be looking for the good in them and loving them with a pure heart. After all, there are reasons why you fell madly in love with this individual. Focus on those qualities and characteristics that melted your heart and caused you to say within your heart, *he or she is the one for me. This is the one that I want to spend the rest of my life with.*

After you honestly surrender your heart to the Lord in prayer, asking Him to both heal your heart and renew it with love and passion for your spouse, then begin to pray that He will help them understand their own heart as well. Hearts can change through the various seasons of marriage, often creating challenging issues to work through. Unfulfilled expectations within the relationship, challenges at work, ongoing financial needs, and countless issues arising in daily life can become problematic and affect your marriage.

This is the perfect time for the two of you to implement an attitude and disposition of "mutual respect" toward one another. Begin to shift your focus away from your wants and needs and establish a new priority. The following life-changing priorities work every time.

- Christ's word and will for my life will now become my top priority... Forever.
- I will place my husband's/wife's desires and needs above my own and acknowledge that my respectful actions and attitudes will help him/her to live life feeling safe, secure, and loved unconditionally.
- I will acknowledge I am a special and unique individual created in the image of God, equal in worth to everyone, however, I will also acknowledge that I have been created and called to serve others just as Christ came to serve all humanity.

These are the same life-changing priorities that were presented to Wayne and Gail. After years of frustration, disappointment, and explosions of anger in their marriage, they were now beginning a new and wonderful season of life. Sure, they would fail occasionally, but they would get back up and refocus on their new priorities and continue to move forward, developing and enjoying the most fulfilling marriage they had ever experienced.

In their personal quest for intimacy, they joined a Bible study with several other couples. They began to discuss ways that they could grow together spiritually. They were finally realizing the importance of developing and sharing a spiritual foundation.

In the next chapter, let's take a look at each of the steps these couples learned that firmly established them in their spiritual lives.

Chapter 3: *Steps to Spiritual Intimacy for Couples*

The first and most important step of all.

The first step toward spiritual intimacy within your marriage begins with an acknowledgment that you have a personal relationship with Christ within *your* heart. It is up to your husband or wife to acknowledge that personal relationship within themselves. If they are not open to a relationship with Christ at this time, you should continue to follow Christ's teachings. As you obey the life-changing words of Christ, the Holy Spirit will work through you to show your unbelieving or doubting spouse what the true love of God looks like in real life. Countless husbands and wives have surrendered their hearts to the truth of God's word because of the loving and pure example set by their spouses. The clearest promise of this truth can be found in 1 Peter 3:1-2, "In the same way, you wives must accept the authority of your husband. Then, even if some refuse to obey the good news, your godly lives will speak to them without any words. They will be won over by observing your pure and reverent lives."

Ladies, trust God even when it is challenging to trust your husband because of his past mistakes and decisions. Be encouraged by the fact that Christ has promised to finish the good work that He has begun in him. This same passage requires men to show the honor and respect that they deserve to their wives. The gospel of Christ promotes more honor and respect for females than any religion I am aware of. This passage continues to say that the inner beauty of a wife is in many ways more important than her outward beauty.

Dr. Jack Hyles wrote a book in the 1960s called, *Let's Go Soul Winning* and he presented these passages from Romans as steps towards a road to salvation. Countless times the "Roman Road to Salvation" has been used in helping individuals to understand God's plan of grace and salvation for them. Please read over these four passages of Scripture before you continue.

Romans 1:16 *"for I am not ashamed of the gospel of Christ, because it is the power of God for the salvation of everyone who believes: first for the Jew, then for the Gentile."* In other words, the gospel, God's word, reveals the power and saving grace that we all need so that we may know Him and receive new hearts. You must believe that His word is true and we should never be ashamed of it.

Romans 3:23 *"For all have sinned and fallen short of the glory of God."* Simply put, none of us deserve to be forgiven of our sins and to be saved.

Romans 5:8 *"But God demonstrates his own love for us in this: that while we were still sinners, Christ died for us."* This passage reveals the incredible truth that Christ died for us while we were still being disobedient to him and deserving of his punishment. He loves you that much.

Romans 6:23 *"for the wages of sin is death, but the gift of God is eternal life in Christ Jesus our Lord."* Talk about amazing grace! He warns us ahead of time that if we reject him and continue in sin our final payment for our rebellious life will be eternal death as well as unnecessary heartache in this life. However, He declares that He has given us a gift of everlasting life in the presence of Jesus Christ who embodies love and is the Prince of peace.

Please write out your prayer of salvation or rededication today.

Now that you have surrendered your heart to God's word or renewed your commitment to follow Him, you can have a sincere discussion with your husband or wife about their beliefs and their relationship with Christ. Of course, you want to support and encourage your spouse but please note: You are not the Holy Spirit and you cannot change their mind or their heart yourself. If your spouse tells you that they are not ready to discuss the subject, then you simply continue to be a faithful follower of Christ and lift them up daily in non-judgmental prayers. And along the way, you should never be condescending to them about your spiritual journey.

I have children and grandchildren who have played in a variety of sporting events, and many of them play or have played basketball. The ACC tournament and the NCAA tournament are like national holidays at our home. Too many times we have seen players "talking junk" to other players only to find out by the end of the game that the one with the loudmouth and arrogant comments was not nearly as good as the other player who was calm and composed.

Even though you may feel as though you are only giving "constructive criticism" because you love them, it still may not be received well, especially if your spouse is already feeling as though they are letting you down and possibly letting the Lord down. This may cause them to have a short fuse and they will not receive your comments well. Your pressure on them will not get you the desired results. Prayer, however, will get the desired results. Simply stated, "no junk talking" to your spouse. By the end of the game of life, you may realize that their spiritual commitment and maturity may have surpassed your own.

Now, with all of this in mind, if you have a husband or wife who is ready to grow in Christ and pursue this extraordinarily fulfilling marriage then let's get started.

Let's begin by gaining a better understanding from our first of several insights on communication.

Chapter 4: *Steps to Spiritual Intimacy - Praying Together ...Out Loud*

Bonding hearts and developing trust in His presence.

Please don't give up on your journey or this book when I suggest that you begin to pray out loud with one another! Allow me to explain before you jump over this section that sounds intimidating or unnecessary in your relationship.

We all can agree that improved communication is one of the most effective ways to create and maintain intimacy in a marriage. Ideas for a couple to develop improved communication skills will be discussed later in the book. However, everyone should understand this truth first.

Prayer is the most sacred and life-changing form of communication known to man.

Praying for your spouse is one of the most caring actions you can participate in. You pray for friends or fellow church members or sometimes even individuals that you have never met because you hear of heartbreaking or challenging situations they are going through. Prayer is an expression of both love and faith. Even when you are only praying for yourself you are expressing "belief" in a God that you "believe" loves you and cares enough for you that He will answer your prayer.

Praying husbands and wives should make a conscious decision that the well-being of their spouse will be at the top of their prayer list for the rest of their lives. As you serve the Lord, you should desire each day for your husband or wife to receive God's richest blessings in their lives. You should rejoice with them when they rejoice and share life's happiest moments and victories together.

When your husband or wife is going through a challenging time, they should know that not only your thoughtful words and presence will be available to them, but that you are also lifting them up to an Almighty God who can bring strength, direction, and blessing to them during difficult seasons of life.

Your desire to pray for your husband or wife will often reflect your deeper personal attitude toward them.

When you do not feel as though they are meeting your needs and bringing you the happiness or fulfillment you feel that you deserve, then you will be faced with a decision. Do you become angry and quit praying for them? Do you find yourself praying self-centered prayers while asking the Lord to punish them or cause them to suffer the way that you feel you are suffering? Or are you maturing to a place where you understand you should ask the Lord to bless them the same way that the Lord is blessing you today?

Let me further explain. We would all be wise to understand that we are in a relationship with the Lord himself. You can love Him, or you can reject him. You can praise His name, or you can curse His name. However, God's Heart always displays His unconditional love towards you. He is blessed and He loves it when you commit your heart and life to showing Him the honor and respect that is due to Him. But admittedly, countless people live a life that shows complete disrespect and an attitude of rejection towards Him. You would think in His anger He would destroy all of those who do not honor Him, after all, He created them to begin with. He doesn't do that though. He continues to look for the good in every individual and motivates them to live a life that reflects His heart. A heart of unconditional love. Simply put, His love is not simply shared with those who show great love, appreciation, and admiration for Him. His love is shared with everyone. Even on the days that Christ's followers disappoint Him and fall back into their old ways and sins, He continues to love them. He loves you today, just the way that you are. That's the way that He wants us to love others. Just the way that they are, knowing that He is the one and the only one who can help them sort through the failures of their past and journey forward in life embracing His healing grace and power. It's not that there are no consequences for disobedience toward the Lord, there certainly are, but he chooses to love everyone until they draw their last breath with His pure love.

When I share about the need for unconditional love towards a spouse, Bill comes to mind. Bill and Joyce had been married for 12 years and they both could write a list a page long of the things they loved about each other and enjoyed doing together, such as countless projects in the house they had completed together and the ongoing yard improvements. They shared an interest in volunteering for the Arts Council and everyone knew how excited they both got as they planned future vacations for the family.

Bill worked very hard in his career and had always dreamed of being successful so that his family could enjoy security and hopefully even a few extra things along the way. There were numerous areas of their relationship that other couples envied. Joyce was grateful that she only had to work part-time, which allowed her time to help her fourth-grade daughter not only with homework but also occasionally volunteer at the school. It also allowed her to spend some time with her friends.

However, Bill began to notice a change in Joyce's behavior. It was as though she was hiding something at times and occasionally her behavior was erratic. Bill could not put his finger on what was going on but he knew that he no longer trusted Joyce the way that he had in the past. He continued to pray for her and would occasionally ask her what was going on. The answer was always the same, "I'm fine, it's only your imagination Bill." Finally, one day while at work, Bill received a call saying that Joyce had not picked up their daughter at school and that he needed to come at once to get her. Bill immediately left work, jumped in his car, and was filled with anxiety as he drove to the school. Of course, he was also concerned about Joyce - why had she not picked up their daughter and was she okay? What could have possibly happened to her? Joyce was not answering her phone, which only increased Bill's anxiety. He arrived at the school and picked up their daughter and quickly drove home. Joyce's car was in the driveway when they arrived and Bill was truly grateful that the family dog was there to greet Caroline, their daughter. He asked her to stay outside, while he went in to check on Joyce. Bill's secret fear was confirmed, Joyce had begun drinking to deal with some anxieties that she was facing in life. Today, however, she had too much to drink and had passed out on the couch. Bill was outraged but he was also brokenhearted.

How could this have possibly happened to Joyce and their family? Bill could have thrown his wife under the bus, so to speak, but he chose to take a snack outside to his daughter and ask her to have a picnic and enjoy the pretty afternoon outdoors. So much within him wanted to become angry and verbally scold Joyce for her behavior. But there was something within his heart that would not allow him to do that. That something was God's grace and forgiving attitude. Bill was wise and did not sweep the situation under the rug. Later, the two of them discussed the event and Joyce showed deep remorse and embarrassment for her actions. They decided to contact a Christian counselor for support and insight into how to deal with their choices concerning their anxieties and fears. During counseling, Bill was shocked to find out how Joyce's father's abandonment of their family still affected the way she processed numerous issues in her life. Scriptures were shared with them as well as methods to process situations that would enable them to move forward as a couple. Bill chose to love his flawed wife unconditionally just as Christ loves him unconditionally every day. And candidly, Bill knew he was not perfect either and Joyce had made the decision and committed time and again to love Bill just as he is.

God's mercies for you are fresh and new today. Are your mercies toward your spouse fresh and new today, or are you carrying yesterday's grudge in your heart against them again today?

Christ loves you unconditionally every day. Do you love your husband or wife unconditionally today? This means that even if you have felt unappreciated again today or that you have not been shown the kindness that you should have received, you will still pray for God's best blessings upon them. You may protest by saying, "I will not be anybody's doormat!" I'm not implying that anyone should become a doormat for another person. However, walking in the humility of Christ is an attitude of the heart, and it's not a demeaning position. If you don't make the decision to love like He loves and to forgive like He forgives, then even if it is not your intention, you will begin to allow deep-rooted bitterness and judgment to grow in your heart. That will always lead to destructive patterns.

Prayer produces intimacy with God and with your spouse.

Prayer creates an atmosphere not only of intimacy, but also of honesty, sincerity, purity, and humility; all extremely important ingredients to a healthy marriage and relationship.

Prayer places you into the presence of God himself, your Creator. It is very difficult to maintain an arrogant, hardhearted, deceiving, or manipulative attitude in His holy presence.

God is love. To abide in His presence is to abide in His love. His love will equip and motivate you to love like He loves. Your spouse benefits from this change in your heart and attitude. You will also benefit from the response that comes from your spouse's heart as you love them unconditionally.

Because of the unrealistic examples that are often portrayed to be the new norm of physical appearance by the media, some husbands or wives find it challenging to even undress in front of one another.

Even though this is often true, someone recently commented to me, "It seems that it is easier to be naked physically in front of each other than to pray together and to show or reveal our hearts to each other." The truth is, that is often the case.

There are many things we can do with or for one another without having a pure heart. However, prayer is an active communication that requires honesty. If a husband or wife prays with a deceptive heart, they most likely will not be able to do it for very long.

The reality is that a wife could cook a full course meal for her husband or even surrender to his sexual desires, and not do any of it with a pure heart or a feeling of loving connection with him. In the same way, a husband could wash his wife's car without being asked and fill it with gas, he could help with other chores that he knows are meaningful to her, yet none of it could be done for the right reasons.

The very nature of prayer begs for sincerity and truth. I would suggest to you that sincere prayer produces a spiritual nakedness or vulnerability within a couple's hearts. To pray with your husband or wife often brings about an openness and truthfulness of heart that a couple has never experienced. It brings about a depth of spiritual intimacy which develops trust and unconditional love within the marriage, as well as laying a solid foundation for both emotional and physical intimacy at its deepest levels.

Prayer becomes a filter for our personal agendas and attitudes.

In Luke 18:1, Christ makes two profound statements:

1. We should always pray
2. We should never give up

Many passages teach the importance of consistent and faithful prayers. However, if there were only this one passage taught by Christ Himself, it should be enough to remind us that in our challenging moments of marriage, the relationship is worth fighting for, and prayer is the tool used to improve it.

Your attitudes bring about far more circumstances than you realize. One scripture that enlightens us on this truth is found in 1 Peter 3:7. Let me make several observations about this one passage:

- Husbands should live with their wives in an understanding manner.
- A wife is deserving of her husband's support and honor.
- Both a husband and wife are equal heirs of God's grace and life.
- A husband's prayers can be hindered because of his attitude toward his wife.

Volumes could be written concerning the difference in the emotional and physical makeup of a husband and wife as well as their different spiritual views. How well do you understand your wife? Some of you are thinking, *I honestly feel as though I understand my wife pretty well.* while others are simply shaking their heads, thinking, *I'm not sure I know her very well at all, or at least, she doesn't think that I do.* Communication will be a key to improving your perception, and this could be the beginning of learning how to communicate at a deeper level.

The last point I will make about this topic is why I believe it is so important to pray out loud. Praying out loud will require you both to come out of your comfort zone. One of you probably feels more at ease to pray out loud depending on your personal prayer life. Or it could be that you grew up in a home where different family members prayed out loud, or you grew up in a church where different individuals had an opportunity to pray out loud. It may be that you are more of an extrovert than your spouse and simply don't find praying out loud as challenging. I often see wives who are spiritually hungry for their family to receive God's best blessings and who have developed an active prayer life, and for this reason, find it easier to pray out loud than their husbands do. I know it is awkward for many men, but I do believe that God has called men to be spiritual leaders. I've told a number of men that if you can scream at a ballgame or constantly discuss business matters with your coworkers, then certainly you should be able to simply talk to God out loud with your wives present.

Wives tell me repeatedly that they are greatly encouraged and strengthened when their husbands pray for them or for their children out loud, either in a couple or family setting. Some wives say it's one of the greatest gifts they've ever received from their husbands. Some words of encouragement, it will not be awkward to pray out loud for very long. Just like any new habit you are developing, the more you do it the easier it becomes. You do not have to pray an eloquent prayer like Billy Graham or your pastor. Simply talk to God. Be honest. Be real. Wives, make sure that you do not do or say anything that will appear degrading to your husband if he is making this effort.

Thank him for it and encourage him and you simply join in the prayer when he is finished. It doesn't matter if you begin with a 30-second or one-minute prayer, start somewhere. If necessary, for a short time the wife could be the one to pray if the husband refuses or wants to work himself into a more comfortable place. However, men, it is your place to lead in this area. You can do it! God is not asking you to do something that you are not capable of doing. Yes, praying together silently is excellent and much better than nothing, but there is a power that comes from praying together out loud that is irreplaceable.

Chapter 5: *Steps to Spiritual Intimacy – Worshiping*

Exalting our Creator together ... as one.

Worship - the feeling or expression of reverence and admiration for a deity. The worship of God.

As Christians, it should become as natural as breathing or eating that we would want to exalt our Creator and our Savior. Our God, who has expressed himself as Father, Son, and Holy Spirit has given us our very breath. Every day when we awake, we enjoy the beauty of His creation, and our ongoing needs are met by His hand of provision. We have disappointed Him and broken His commandments countless, countless times, and yet His forgiveness and grace remain as His ongoing gift to His children. Our praise and worship should be our gift to Him. You are called and created to praise and worship the Lord.

Psalm 96:1–9

Oh, sing to the Lord a new song!

Sing to the Lord, all the earth.

Sing to the Lord, bless His name;

Proclaim the good news of His salvation from day to day.

Declare His glory among the nations,

His wonders among all peoples.

The Lord is great and greatly to be praised;

He is to be feared above all gods.

For all the gods of the people are idols,

But the Lord made the heavens.

Honor and majesty are before Him;

Strength and beauty are in His sanctuary.

<u>Give to the Lord, all families of all peoples,</u>

<u>Give to the Lord Glory and strength.</u>

<u>Give to the Lord the glory due His name;</u>

<u>Bring an offering, and come into His courts.</u>

<u>Oh, worship the Lord in the beauty of holiness!</u>

Tremble before Him, all the earth.

Also, let me share just a few verses from **Psalms 95:1-3 & 6-7**

Oh come, let us sing to the Lord!

<u>Let us shout joyfully to the rock of our salvation.</u>

<u>Let us come before His presence with thanksgiving;</u>

<u>Let us shout joyfully to Him with psalms.</u>

For the Lord is great and the great King above all gods.

Oh come, <u>let us worship and bow down;</u>

<u>Let us kneel before the Lord our maker.</u>

For He is our God, and we are the people of His pasture,

And the sheep of His hand.

PLEASE don't see this as boring Scripture and skip right over it. God calls you to understand these principles and to participate in this act of worship with a pure and sincere heart. I would like to make several points about worship and then we will discuss how it both applies to you and your spouse and how it connects your hearts together.

"Oh come, let us sing to the Lord." This is an action phrase that requires you to do something. Nowhere does it indicate that this can be a passive participation when you are having a good day or a little extra time? No! The Scripture is inspired to call us out of our personal preferences and agendas and to participate in a higher calling.

"Sing to the Lord!" This has far more to do with the purity and the sincerity of your heart than it does with the quality of your voice.

"Shout joyfully to the rock of our salvation!" Shout with joy, acknowledging that your salvation is on a firm foundation, the rock.

Families are called to give glory and honor to the Lord.

Be grateful when you enter the presence of the Lord. Stop your constant or ongoing complaining about things that have not changed to this point or that you are currently frustrated about. He has already blessed our lives so much that if we had 100 more lifetimes, we could still not adequately thank Him and praise Him for what He has already done for us.

Acknowledge that He is not only a god, He is "the true and great God" above all lesser gods and deities that try to steal His majesty and glory. As I have traveled in different countries of the world spreading the gospel, I have seen countless people worship the sun, moon, rivers, and animals. I have also seen many people, even in our communities, worship the personal appearance of a spouse, their child, a financial portfolio, or the dream home and sports cars they drive. Technically, we can say that anything that one exalts above the true God Himself is an idol.

We are to be humble in His presence and bow down as we worship. This could be physically bowing down or simply an attitude of the posture of our heart. Yes, we are to kneel before the Lord, our maker.

Acknowledge that we are His children and He has created us for His divine purpose.

Lastly, but of great importance, we are instructed to proclaim the good news of His salvation every day we live and declare His glory among the nations of the world as we have the opportunity to - <u>with our efforts beginning at home.</u>

So, let's acknowledge the following truths. Worship is a state or attitude of one's heart.

Worship is mandated by God Himself.

Worship allows an ordinary person to exalt the Almighty God by offering Him praise for His countless means of provision and blessing for their life. As an individual praises the Lord, their hope and joy are greatly renewed which has a deep impact on their attitude, outlook on life, as well as their problems and concerns. It also reminds the worshiper that the Almighty God whom they are lifting up is more than adequate to take care of any needs, problems, or fears that they could be facing in their lives. Including ANY marriage problems.

God understands beyond anyone the importance of a husband and wife walking in agreement as they maneuver through the many challenges and temptations in this world. He knows emphatically that they must be on the same page and that their hearts be as one instead of living two different lifestyles to obtain two different goals. If a husband has a heart to pursue the Lord, yet his wife has a heart to pursue a more self-centered life that includes pleasing herself and enjoying the ongoing parties and activities of this world, there will be problems.

If a wife has surrendered her heart to the Lord and deeply yearns to honor Christ with her life, her money, and her influence over her children, yet her husband sees no value in acknowledging God, there will be issues. If he feels his income is more than adequate to take care of the family's needs and views everyone in the family as healthy and doing well in school etc., he may choose to set his own standard for what is right and wrong. He may even exalt his own achievements, failing to realize that it is God's grace that has given him the ability to achieve what he has.

This leads me to a heartbreaking scenario that has been experienced by many and shared with me over and over again.

2 Corinthians 6:14 "do not be unequally yoked together with unbelievers. For what fellowship has righteousness with unrighteousness? And what communion has light with darkness?"

There is a dilemma I have seen numerous times when someone has committed their heart to follow Christ and His teachings, yet they are in a relationship with someone who does not believe in Christ or who refuses to take His word seriously. To clarify, these statements should help explain what leads to the dilemma. Will you be a person who tends to get even with others or to forgive their offenses? Can you make money on a shady deal as long as it does not seemingly hurt you or anyone you love, even though you know the basis of the transaction is dishonest? How about tithing? Could you allow your wife to give offerings to a church or children on the mission field when you want to use that money for a truck payment or possibly a fishing boat that you've worked hard for?

These are very real questions that can have a major impact on the relationship. I have seen loving wives bend over backward, trying to meet the needs of their husbands. Husbands who give little to no time to church attendance or to develop a deeper relationship with the Lord. I have seen such dedicated wives break down crying uncontrollably because their husbands would actually threaten them in some manner if they tried to give even a small portion of their own earnings to a local church or mission work. I have seen women so hungry to worship the Lord and come early to assist and participate in any way they could at the church, knowing that they would need to leave 20 or 30 minutes before the service ended on Sunday so that they could get home and have her husband's meal on the table shortly after noon on Sunday.

It's hard to believe that some husbands could have such resentment toward their wives' joy and excitement about being at church that they would intentionally demand that they be back home to serve them lunch at a certain time, even when there were no activities planned or work schedules to meet. Acts of control, jealousy, and manipulation coming from a selfish heart can often crush the spirit and joy of marriage within their spouse. Extreme cases? Possibly so, however, I have witnessed this many times over the years.

Or possibly a believing wife has put money aside for weeks or months to be able to bless orphans at Christmas. However, her husband finds that money that had been saved and feels justified in going on an unexpected golfing trip with his friends because, in his mind, he is the one who hates his job and works hard to earn it. One wants to have family prayer, while the other wants to watch an X-rated movie. One wants to go to church, while the other wants to sleep in again this Sunday. These situations can be very stressful and, over the years, take a horrible toll on the hearts and minds of wonderful people.

If both husband and wife would only realize that we have been created in God's image and He has called all of us to surrender our hearts to Him in a manner that would change our value system from constantly being about us, to instead living for Him. As we live for Him, we will learn to be thankful to Him. We will have a heart to worship Him and acknowledge that He is our great provider of all our material needs as well as our mental and spiritual health and well-being. He is the Prince of peace and the one who gives us the deepest levels of contentment and courage to move forward as we face life's obstacles and challenges.

Now there are two equally important truths for you to acknowledge and embrace.

Number one, as I have mentioned numerous times, you must acknowledge that you have been called to worship with the variety of expressions that God has provided for you as a believer as an ongoing part of your life and relationship with him.

Number two, God has called you to embrace a life of worship that will help you motivate and inspire your wife or husband, as well as your children, to become sincere, God-loving, God-fearing worshipers of our Almighty God themselves.

The peace that you obtain in your heart as you walk with Christ can and will help establish an atmosphere of safety and security within your marriage and home. Your relationship as a worshiper will also cause you to reflect the purity and holiness of the nature of God himself.

When you spend time with someone, you will most definitely be influenced by them. Spending time in the presence of the Lord changes us from being selfish, personally fulfilling individuals into those who are more caring and concerned about others.

I believe that when you stand before the Lord at the end of your life you will give an account to Him for the way that you have encouraged and enabled your husband or wife to understand, embrace, and grow in the word of God and how you supported them in becoming the man or the woman that God created them to be. Or you may be judged for the way that you hindered your spouse from fulfilling their calling and purpose because of your personal agenda, coupled with your pride and arrogance. Or you may be judged for allowing the pleasures of this world to drown out the insight into the indescribable pleasures and joys that the Lord had in store for you eternally and even in this world once they were surrendered to him.

How personal is worship? Consider these passages.

Ephesians 3:17 <u>so that Christ may dwell "in your hearts" through faith</u>. And I pray that you will be rooted and grounded in love.

2 Corinthians 13:5 "Examine yourselves to see if your faith is genuine; test yourselves. <u>Surely you know that Jesus Christ is among you, if not, you have failed the test of genuine faith."</u>

Galatians 2:20 "My old self has been crucified with Christ. It is no longer I who live, <u>but Christ lives in me.</u>

Colossians 1:27 "To them God willed to make known what are the riches of the glory of this mystery among the Gentiles: <u>which is Christ in you, the hope of glory.</u>

In other words, you and Christ are one through faith and the commitment that you have made to one another. Does that level of oneness sound familiar? Yes, in one other place marriage.

It's crucial not to leave out the very important topic of children and how they fit into the topic of worship. When a couple has children, a love is formed that we have never experienced before. That love will truly melt your heart with joy and happiness. Scripture clearly teaches that children are a gift from the Lord and that parents who have a house full of children find strength and blessing.

Psalms 127:3 "Behold, children are a heritage from the Lord, the fruit of the womb is a reward."

Parents should wholeheartedly love, protect, and provide for their children and train them in the way of the Lord. Children are to be nurtured, trained, and prepared for a life that honors Christ and represents him in the next generation.

However, Scripture does not say that a parent is supposed to "become one" with their child even though we all can certainly relate to that depth of love toward our children. A husband and wife's loving expression of oneness toward each other should be an example before their children of how they should both love and be loved in their adult relationship of marriage if they choose to marry, or how to walk honorably and biblically in a single lifestyle.

Too often, parents develop an unscriptural relationship with their children. Many young parents are trying to live out their dreams through their children or due to their own issues with fear or insecurities, they find themselves hovering over their children in an unhealthy manner. Because of their behavior, their sons and daughters cannot develop properly into the young men and women God intended for them to be. They grow up lacking the skills to cope with the challenges of life or to make decisions on their own. These children often grow up developing into needy or insecure adults.

Another scenario is husbands and wives who have just been hanging on by a thread in their marriage and wake up in an empty home without purpose and love. The empty nest syndrome often comes much quicker than couples are prepared for. It is truly an adjustment for any couple who has had a child in their home for 18 years or longer.

I constantly encourage couples to find at least a few dollars regularly that they use to continue to date, share their interests and dreams with one another, as well as keep the fires and passion of love alive throughout the busy and sometimes exhausting years of raising their children.

Love and worship God individually for your own well-being. Love and worship God as a couple to grow together in Christ and as an example to your children. Love and worship God as a family so your children will know the personal blessings of the Lord and grow up knowing family worship is a normal and accepted practice in a Christian home.

Even though a large portion of your love, finances, and time will go into raising your children, they cannot become the object of your worship. Nor should children take away your personal focus from worshiping your worthy and Almighty God or dividing the two of you as a couple as you worship together.

Chapter 6: *Steps to Spiritual Intimacy – Becoming One through Inspirational Truths*

Like-minded thoughts create unity.

I can almost hear a collective gasp from many readers asking, "Does this author realize he's asking us to do something else? Doesn't he know how early we are getting up just to leave for work and the frantic pace we keep throughout the day as we continually schedule and reschedule carpooling to our children's classes as well as their practices, not counting their competitions and games?" You may not be in a season of life where you are sharing your time and energy taking care of children, but it may be something else like you are now taking care of your parents. As you get older, you will clearly see that there are different seasons of life. Possibly you are in a season where there is a need for ongoing repairs on your home, or perhaps health issues require constant attention that seem to absorb not only your money but your time and sometimes even your joy. Regardless of the reasons, your schedule is simply tight. But yes, I do understand.

One of the beautiful benefits of having personal devotions as well as sharing them as a couple is that it does not have to take a lot of your time or require you to reschedule important responsibilities and deadlines you are already confronted with.

<u>*Daily devotions can enable you to develop an inspiring thought that helps bring you peace throughout your day or a word of wisdom and direction that helps you make wise decisions.*</u>

Daily devotions are a wonderful reminder in the midst of your busy and sometimes chaotic life that you are devoted to both God and His word. Devotionals that are written with marriage and relationships in mind often encourage a husband or wife to pray over their spouse or possibly to look for the good in them on a day that they are feeling somewhat unloved themselves, for example. Biblical truths are often the tool that the Lord uses to direct our thinking and heal our hearts.

Let me ask you this, is a negative thought that enters your mind as you are getting ready in the morning, or possibly an alarming or upsetting event that is broadcast on TV as you are going out the door, going to be the foundation for your thought process throughout the day? If so, how will this affect your faith walk? And yes, not only your faith walk and attitude toward Christ, but also toward your spouse?

Will your short conversation over the phone during the workday with your spouse reflect frustration, fear, or even hopelessness? Just like yourself, your spouse wants and needs a word of loving encouragement, hope, and inspiration. In addition, you both want to feel respected and appreciated.

Devotions can be the foundation for all of these positive contributions to your heart, your marriage, and more.

<u>Sharing and becoming one is at the core of marriage and relationships. Why not share uplifting insights from Scripture or even from someone's life experiences with one another as a means of encouragement and support?</u>

Mark had commented more than once that when he was in high school and trade school, he was required to read, but now that he had graduated no one was going to tell him what to read. Besides, he didn't enjoy reading. Training manuals for his job and his monthly subscription to *Outdoor World* were all the printed material he wanted around.

Mark was young in his faith and had not yet learned the importance of being strengthened by God's word or receiving the wisdom that it contains. Daily devotions were seen to him as unnecessary and a waste of time. He assumed he could get enough encouragement during church on Sunday to help him through life and keep the Lord satisfied with him. However, an unfortunate scenario occurred in Mark's life that radically changed his view on daily devotions. Or was it a "fortunate" event? Mark would soon see as the days unfolded.

Mark was unexpectedly fired from his job. A job that he loved and offered him a promising future. His playful, youthful attitude outweighed his sense of maturity, responsibility, and commitment to the company and one day he violated a company policy while on the clock. A policy that carried a zero-tolerance mandate with it.

Even though the head of the HR department had liked Mark since the day that he met and hired him, he explained to him in an unapologetic tone that there were no excuses or acceptable explanations for his behavior. Mark felt humiliated as he was walked to the gate by a member of the security force, who was also a friend of his.

Mark got in his car for the ride home knowing that he was going to have to explain this costly mistake to his wife. How was he going to explain this foolish action and its consequences on their family? In addition, they had just purchased a new truck only three months earlier.

Mark had heard Linda snap at him with harsh criticisms many times over the years of their marriage. Linda had admitted that she had unresolved issues of anger in her heart, but it just seemed as though there were times Mark pushed the right buttons, which caused her to say or do things that she would feel ashamed of. Mark really dreaded going home and thought about riding around for hours just to think and sort things out in his mind. However, on that day, Mark knew that Linda was supposed to call him during his break time to discuss their evening plans. She was going to know something was wrong anyway, so he decided to go home and face her wrath and criticism.

When Mark walked in the front door, Linda came to greet him, but her expression was one of shock. "What are you doing at home?" she asked. "Are you sick?" Mark uttered that yes, he genuinely did feel sick, real sick, but not because of something like a virus or the flu. About to fall apart himself, Mark looked at his wife and blurted out, "I lost my job. They fired me today." It was as though his comments sucked the air out of the room. Linda sat down in shock and asked, "Why, what did you do this time?" Oh, how Mark wanted to run and just leave the room but he knew he had to stay and face the music. The tone of her voice let him know that she may rip him apart the way that she had done so many times in the past. She sat there squirming as Mark explained the whole situation and he ended by saying that there were no excuses. "I did wrong and I'm very sorry for it. I don't know how, but I'm going to make this up to you." So many crazy thoughts were swirling around in Linda's mind. She felt like telling him off and telling him he needed to grow up! Honestly, she felt enough frustration that she could have walked across the room and started beating him on the arm, but she didn't.

To her great surprise, she began to feel an unusual calmness in her heart that didn't even make sense to her. Why wasn't she exploding and telling Mark off the way she had done so many times over the years? When the shock of Mark's announcement wore off Linda caught herself trying to understand why she felt this calmness and then it came to her, *it's what I read this morning and prayed about during my devotion time!*

Could that 10 minutes I spent alone with the Lord this morning actually be changing my whole attitude right now while Mark is giving me such devastating news? Yes, it "actually" was. You see, Linda's devotion that particular morning had been based on a passage of Scripture found in Philippians chapter 4: 4-7. This passage encourages believers by saying, *"Rejoice in the Lord always. I will say it again; rejoice! Let your gentleness be evident to all. The Lord is near. Do not be anxious about anything, but in everything, by prayer and petition, with thanksgiving, present your requests to God. And the peace of God, which transcends all understanding, will guard your hearts and your minds in Christ Jesus."*

Just a coincidence? Was this a miracle or at least a divinely orchestrated moment that provided peace, strength, and guidance during a potentially catastrophic moment in their lives?

While Mark wasn't trying to be funny, he later stated," Yeah, it was a miracle that Linda didn't verbally rip my head off and make me feel like a failure like she usually does."

Linda began to sense something happening inside her heart and mind that she had never experienced. It was the presence of the Lord in the midst of one of the most difficult and challenging days of her life.

Scripture boldly states that God's word is alive and powerful. God's word was not only given to the Old Testament patriarchs or the New Testament disciples and apostles. God gave his word to you and me. His words are life-changing right now in the midst of your life and your generation.

Linda had only gone to a ladies' prayer group just a few times, but she knew some things in her life needed to change. However, the built-up anger and frustration in her life not only disappointed and offended Mark, but she was disappointed and fed up with herself. Sometimes, she didn't even know why she felt such anxiety within herself and why, all too often, she had such a short fuse and temper. So when one of the ladies at church had been thoughtful enough to invite her to their morning prayer group, she was reluctant because she was a little shy, but she decided that something had to change, and it was worth a try. In the prayer group, she had heard a couple of the ladies making comments about the Lord speaking to their hearts through Scripture or even changing circumstances in their marriage or home. Linda wondered how this could be possible, but she continued to go to the meetings and, at their encouragement, had begun daily devotions herself.

What timing! Had the Lord known two months in advance before Mark was fired that they would be in this situation and need extra encouragement, insight, and wisdom to be able to survive the storm in their life and marriage? Yes, He most certainly did. And His great grace had been preparing Linda's heart for this day even though she did not realize it.

Just consider the passage that she read that very morning.

The passage reminded Linda of the importance of rejoicing, not only rejoicing but *rejoicing always*. And yes, *rejoicing always* means during all the various situations in our life, whether it be a time of great blessing or great trial. When Scripture encourages us to rejoice, it's because we have confidence in the life, death, and resurrection power of Jesus Christ our Lord. His power is greater than any of our trials. Rejoicing becomes a heartfelt declaration that He is our Lord and He will strengthen us and enable us to walk through any situation in life with victory, peace, and deep joy in our hearts.

Linda had also felt convicted in her heart when she read over the portion of the Scripture that said, let your gentleness be evident to everyone. Just that morning, she sat at her kitchen table reading the Scripture and it jumped out at her as to how meaningful it would be to her husband if she would have more gentleness in her attitude toward him instead of criticism. She honestly had even prayed about that and asked God to change her heart.

However, the portion of the Scripture that especially challenged Linda during her devotions was the part that said, (Philippians 4:6) *"Do not be anxious about anything."* Really? So God is telling me not to be anxious about anything, why would He even say that?

The truth is that in our day-to-day life and especially when we are going through very emotional and challenging times, we often look at life through tunnel vision. We only see what's happening and sense the emotions of the moment. However, God stands back, seeing the entire picture of your life. Incredibly, the entire picture from before you were even born to your eternal future. He sees it all. He's never been worried, He's never been afraid, and there's never been a situation in world history that He hasn't had an answer for those who would take the time to ask Him. Sometimes we have to wait patiently, but our Lord is not one who plays guessing games or strings his children along. He knows your heart, He knows your needs, and He knows how to heal your heart and meet your needs. Every time!

Jeremiah 29:11 says, "For I know the thoughts that I think toward you, says the Lord, thoughts of peace and not of evil, to give you a future and a hope." Additionally, the passage says that when we "call upon the Lord with all of our heart, He will answer us."

Linda's devotions had also told her to bring all of her requests and needs to God in an attitude of prayer, with thanksgiving. That made sense when she read it at the kitchen table with no chaos in her life, but now as Mark sat in front of her saying that he had lost his job and they had payments due with no guarantee of another job, the Lord is asking her to pray with an attitude of thanksgiving? Is that possible and could she even bring herself to do that?

There was no way for Linda to explain the emotions that she continued to experience as the two of them sat discussing all that had happened at work and its effect on their future. Linda sat there quietly for so long that Mark honestly became genuinely concerned. He kept asking her to say something and she just sat there. Linda was at a crossroads that she had never encountered in her life. Finally, to Mark's surprise, she calmly looked at him and said, "Just be quiet, I need a minute to think this through. I am hurt, and I am shocked, but for some reason, I'm feeling like everything will be okay." Mark replied, "What? I was afraid that you would tell me again how big of a failure I am or that you want me to leave." He thought Linda was in a state of shock or depression, but rather, she was just in a moment of deep, deep thought. She was trying to figure out how God's word could honestly apply to their lives and their marriage, or if it was even possible.

They took a short break and got something to drink, and Linda walked outside on the back porch for a few minutes and stood there in the sunshine and prayed. Then she went back inside and asked Mark to sit down at the kitchen table with her. Then something happened for the first time in their marriage. Was it a coincidence? Was it a miracle or divine intervention? You can call it what you want to, but it changed the course of their marriage and their future and may have saved the marriage as well.

They began to have a meaningful conversation. Unlike previous conversations, especially when they were upset or had a problem, this time, there was no screaming. There were no demeaning comments or blame. What an unusual but wonderful conversation they were having! For several minutes Mark kept waiting for the verbal dagger and insult, but it never came. As Linda began to share with Mark how the Scripture became meaningful and real in her heart and her mind, it made Mark start thinking. Something had undeniably happened in Linda because it was like a different woman was sitting at the kitchen table. Mark wasn't accustomed to Linda speaking so calmly when they had a problem.

Somehow, during this conversation, Linda was able to express the truth that she was angry, hurt, and disappointed, but it did not stop there. She was also able to express the fact that she loved Mark and knew that he would never intentionally hurt her like that or put their future in jeopardy. Strangely, after Linda shared everything in her heart, Mark felt both loved and respected by his wife. Now, even his heart was changing, and his mind was having different thoughts. More than ever Mark was utterly determined to succeed and to bless this woman who was standing with him and supporting him in one of his darkest hours.

It was true, Linda had never responded like this. She had never acted so Christ-like in the midst of adversity.

Honestly, Linda did not need to tell Mark that he had failed. He already knew that.

In my experience, few women understand how much a man hates to fail and how deeply it grinds on his mind and heart. Sometimes, our wounds as men are self-inflicted, we have to admit that. Nonetheless, God has placed something in every man's heart to succeed. Too many times during a crisis, wives (whether it be consciously or unconsciously) make comments that belittle and hinder their husband's spiritual and emotional growth and success. Husbands and wives have a mandate from God to live and act in such a way as to encourage and inspire each other to succeed, including when they fall short or experience failures.

The foundation for deeply united hearts with unconditional love and intimacy is birthed in the knowledge and acceptance of God's word and plan for your lives.

Mark and Linda experienced another first that day. They prayed together… out loud.

Mark started by telling the Lord how sorry he was for hurting his wife, as well as letting down his boss and coworkers. He found himself asking the Lord to help him grow up and mature and be the man that he was supposed to be. He prayed for a new beginning and wisdom to get it right next time. He asked the Lord to please, please give him a new job that would provide for his family.

Linda began her part of the prayer time by honestly telling the Lord that she had no idea why she had peace in her heart when she knew that she normally would be angry and vocal. She thanked the Lord for that peace and asked Him to help her understand how His principles work in their lives. She admitted that she didn't know how to rejoice in a time like this but told Him that if He would show her how she would do her best to do it. Then she closed her prayer by asking the Lord to help Mark find a new job and that he would help them spend their money wisely.

During the upcoming days, Mark sent out many resumes and put up a prayer with each one that God's will would be done. More than ever, Mark genuinely wanted to work with a company where he could use his skills and gifts and find a solid career path. No one contacted Mark during that first week and he sometimes felt discouragement as thoughts of being a failure would come back to his mind. He became more hopeful as he entered the second week of sending resumes out, but day after day, with no response, he found himself in a true battle. He felt like a failure, he felt angry, he felt disappointed, and sometimes he even felt like the rules at his former company were unfair. Those first few mornings that Mark sat at his desk sending out his resumes, he observed that Linda continued regularly with her devotions.

One morning in particular, he noticed how calm and peaceful she looked while she was reading a few verses of Scripture that were connected to her devotion. He knew that she was fighting worry and anxiety about their bills, and he had also seen evidence that she had been looking for a job herself, which made him feel guilty. Each time something like that would happen inwardly, he would beat himself up again for letting her down. He thought to himself, *what if, just what if... these devotions are truly helping her. Is this for real and something I should do myself?* A man who had always seen devotions as a waste of time was now in a personal situation where he had to at least consider the possibility that devotions are helpful for everyone, including himself.

It was on Tuesday morning of the third week of unemployment that Mark received a phone call. The call was not about employment, it was about fishing. Pop was a retired gentleman at their church. Everyone loved Pop, who had such an easy-going demeanor and a positive outlook on life. Everyone also knew that Pop loved to fish. If he wasn't helping with a project at the church or manicuring his beautiful lawn, he may well be on the water. Pop was going fishing at one of his favorite places the next morning and asked Mark to go with him. Mark loved to fish and rarely had an opportunity to go with anyone who owned a boat. However, he felt guilty going fishing and having fun when he had not worked in over two weeks. He was so torn he could not even give Pop an immediate answer but told him he would call him back.

Guilt and shame are strong and crippling emotions. They affect countless people in their day-to-day attitudes and actions, but this was a new quandary that Mark had rarely experienced in his life. Linda heard the phone ring and asked Mark who it was, he told her that it was Pop and explained the situation. He went on to tell her how badly he felt about even thinking about having fun at a time like this.

Well, Linda simply continued to surprise Mark at every turn. Not long ago, she would have been screaming at him and saying something like, "No, you certainly don't deserve to have any fun, not with all the pain and heartache you've brought to our family!" But she didn't say anything like that, but instead encouraged him to go with Pop. She reminded Mark that he had done countless projects around the house in the last two weeks and had sent out over 30 resumes. She smiled, "Who knows? Maybe a company will be looking at your resume tomorrow while you are enjoying some time with Pop. And besides, you love fishing and have not been for a long time." With that decision made, Mark contacted Pop and accepted the offer. Honestly, he could hardly sleep that night as he was so excited to go.

The next morning, bright and early, Pop came by the house and picked Mark up. They grabbed a biscuit at a fast-food restaurant and headed straight to the lake putting the boat in the water about sunrise. Pop had more than enough equipment for the two of them to use. He helped Mark get the correct lure tied on and the two of them began trolling through various coves. It had been a while since Mark had fished and he got his line hung up more than once on tree limbs in the water. He was a little embarrassed by that, but Pop had a great attitude and reminded him of the importance of enjoying the day the Lord had given them. As expected, Pop caught the first bass which weighed in at around 3 pounds. In that same cove, Pop caught another one, and finally, Mark caught a couple of fish.

The sun was now up, and it was starting to get warmer, and the view was absolutely beautiful. It was so relaxing, and the two of them found themselves having a very enjoyable time. Mark enjoyed laughter that he had not experienced in weeks. Mid-morning, they tied the boat off in a quiet cove to take a break. Pop opened his cooler and they both found some drinks and snacks to enjoy. Having enjoyed their snacks and with the temperature changing, Pop thought it might be a good idea to change the type of lures they were using. He opened his tackle box and began to make careful selections for both of them. Mark noticed a little book in his tackle box, you could tell that it was worn and had even had some water hit it and curled the pages. The little book looked pretty beaten up, and out of curiosity, Mark asked him what it was. Pop responded that it was his devotional book. With a grin, Pop said it was written for fishermen. Mark said, "You have to be kidding, a devotional book written for fishermen?" He was genuinely surprised because this entire devotional conversation was so new to him. Pop told him that he had carried it with him for many years. He said, "I have read through it time and time again. When I'm here on the water, I love the boat ride, of course, I love the challenge of choosing the correct lures or bait given different weather patterns, and I love catching fish. But look around, Mark. This is a huge and beautiful lake. We've seen countless unspoiled acres and even watched some wildlife moving around the shores coming to get a drink this morning. Mark, my favorite thing about being out here is enjoying God's creation and having time to worship without the distractions I face back home. This devotional book is simple to read and doesn't take but a few minutes, but each story and the Scripture that accompanies it reminds me what life is really all about. It's not just about me having a good time, it's about me serving the One who created me and put me on this earth to start with."

"Mark, I did not bring you out here to preach to you today. I just felt like you needed some time to relax and hopefully laugh a little bit. But you asked about my book, so let me just read today's devotion."

Pop opened the book with its worn pages and began reading, "Matthew 4:18-20 says, 'and Jesus, walking by the sea of Galilee, saw two brothers, Simon called Peter, and Andrew his brother, casting a net into the sea; for they were fishermen. And he said to them, *Follow me, and I will make you fishers of men*. And immediately they left their nets and followed him.'"

He continued with the book's commentary, "*How encouraging! Men who love the serenity of the water and the excitement of catching fish just like you do became some of the most greatly used men of God that Scripture tells us about. Men, ordinary men just like you and me, had their entire lives and hearts changed after they met Christ. Some of these guys had rough edges and bad attitudes. Peter was a man's man who sometimes ran his mouth more than he should, and sometimes it got him into trouble. Christ was even firm with Peter when he would correct his attitudes or actions, but he did his best to receive the correction so he could become a better person. When you find it challenging to believe that God has created you and has a special calling for your life, consider these men. Simple, hard-working fishermen trying to provide for their families as they toiled in the hot sun, harsh winds, and sometimes stormy waters. God saw a potential in them that they did not even see in themselves. The truth is, God also sees great potential in you. Slow down and spend a few minutes praying, just talking to the Lord and asking him what His plan is for your life. When these men understood God's plan for them, they immediately followed His plan and His will. Will you do the same?"*

"Well, what do you think, son? I don't know about you, but those words hit me deep in my heart. We did not even spend 10 minutes reading that Scripture and the comments about it, but I promise you I will not be able to get away from that question. Have I truly surrendered my heart and life to Christ and His will for me? I sure hope I have."

As Pop began to crank up the motor to pull out of the cove, he looked at Mark and said, "You know, that's really all that matters in life." The two men fished until lunch but as the sun heated the water temperature, it was time to go home. The two of them had shared a great day and had put fish in the boat for an enjoyable meal. Once he was back home, Mark went into the house and got cleaned up. Linda had gone to the store, but when she returned, she heard about every minute of their enjoyable morning. Mark spoke wishfully, "Maybe one day we'll have a boat too." Linda looked at him and shook her head, "Hopefully, we will still have a truck to tow it with." They both had a good laugh. Linda later explained that she'd had to use some of their savings that day to pay a couple of bills and buy groceries, but rather than argue, they both were grateful the money had been put aside for an emergency. That evening while enjoying a fish dinner with all the trimmings, Mark shared with Linda about Pop's little book and their devotion for the day. From that day forward, the skeptical, hard-working, tough guy who had never seen the need to make time for devotions decided that it would be a part of his life moving forward.

The next morning Mark got up and read some Scripture and had a time of prayer. He did this the next several mornings even though, honestly, sometimes it was becoming very difficult because there was still no job, and besides, if God was hearing his prayers, He certainly hadn't answered them yet. It can be challenging to learn to trust the Lord and to understand the principle that "His timing is not our timing and that His will is not our will", but it is always correct. There will never be a day that the plan of God for your life is not good. He may be trying to show you or teach you things that you do not even realize you need to know or hear.

Sunday morning, Mark and Linda went to church and thoroughly enjoyed the songs during worship time. They truly needed the encouragement and reminder of God's love and presence in their lives, and both teared up at one point during worship. Partially because of the joy they were sensing but also because of the desperation of their need for a job. Weeks had passed by. The pastor's message on faith and hope certainly hit home in both of their hearts, and they refused to give up. Ironically, Mark's devotion Monday morning was also on faith. Believing in God and learning to trust Him even when you are not seeing anything change was the message Mark was hearing at church Sunday and challenged with during his devotions. Mark was inspired and began to thank the Lord for the job that "he would receive". Mark's faith was now beginning to truly believe that God was hearing his prayers and genuinely cared about him and his family.

Wednesday afternoon, *the* phone call finally came from one of the resumes that had been sent out two weeks earlier. Mark and Linda did a happy dance in the kitchen and became very excited about the interview that was to take place Friday morning. Mark was thrilled, "Are you kidding me, Linda? This isn't just a job, this would be my dream job!" Well, the rest is history, Mark began his dream job the next Monday. He became an exceptional employee and one who had a wonderful attitude and displayed character and maturity. He would tell you himself that much of that change began the day he started doing daily devotions. That was over 7 years ago, and he would not even consider stopping it now.

Chapter 7: *Steps to Spiritual Intimacy*

Fulfillment and Oneness through Serving Others Together.

Mark 10:43-45 *"But among you, it will be different. Whoever wants to be a leader among you must be your servant, and whoever wants to be first among you must be the slave of everyone else. For even the Son of Man came not to be served but to serve others and to give his life as a ransom for many."*

Galatians 5:13b *"...serve one another in love."*

There are many passages that show us clearly what the Lord's plan is for all of us. His plan reveals that we are to serve Him as well as to serve others. Honestly, we all want to be served and to have our wants and needs catered to by others. Frankly, it is a wonderful feeling when someone recognizes a desire or need within our life and makes a special effort to meet that need, which in turn makes us feel appreciated and loved. An expression of support can even lift a heavy burden from our lives. These things are especially appreciated when they come from a loving husband or wife for no apparent reason, just because.

Perhaps the only thing that can make a person feel better than being blessed, is to be the one who saw a need in someone else 's life and blessed them. Most of you can relate to a time and particular circumstance when you saw someone in need, and there was simply something inside your heart that told you to go the extra mile to bless this person. Maybe there was someone in a grocery store line in front of you and their debit card was declined due to lack of funds, and you immediately asked if you could pay for them. The embarrassed and discouraged individual left that store feeling as though somebody cared about them, and possibly even God had just worked a miracle for them so their family could eat. However, you walked to your car with a special feeling in your heart. It was probably a deep feeling of joy and happiness that you had done something for someone else. You had shared some of the money you could have spent on yourself, but the joy of helping that person made you feel so blessed that you wondered why you didn't do things like that more often!

I can't help but think about Ron, one of the men at the church who has quite a few tools and is a good handyman. He certainly hasn't forgotten how good it made him feel when he got a call to help a family last summer. One of the gentlemen at the church had been in a bad car accident and was going to be confined to a wheelchair for a few months during rehab. Ron got the call to help build a ramp leading up to his front door. After a full day's work, he went home that evening hot, sweaty, and exhausted but with one of the most satisfying feelings in his heart that he had ever experienced. It was the satisfaction of knowing that he had done something for someone else. Ron had served someone else rather than being served, and he will never be able to forget the deep sense of contentment and personal satisfaction that it brought to his heart. How could he forget the moment as he walked to his truck and turned back to look at the injured brother and his wife who both had tear-filled eyes thanking him for his help?

Husbands are called to serve the Lord as well as others. And of course, wives are called to serve the Lord as well as others. Why would we think for one moment that all our acts of service would only be shared individually? Of course, some acts of service will be done individually because of the nature of the gifts and the need. However, I challenge you as a couple to understand the importance of both serving the Lord and serving others together, as a team who are one at heart.

Most of the opportunities and ways that we will serve as couples will take place within our church or community. Also, most local churches offer their members opportunities to be a part of either domestic or foreign mission outreaches. I will share much more about that later. However, I cannot help but think about a dear couple that I met around 1978. We were, of course, younger in our lives and ministries at that time. Often when I felt I needed to get away to be alone to think and pray without distractions, I would go to a Christian retreat in the mountains of North Carolina. A precious lady had purchased 700 acres on top of a mountain and, over the years, built a wonderful

Christian retreat. Since it was only one and a half hours away from my home, I often went there for one to four days through the week when very few people would be there, and I got to know the staff very well. I spent countless hours with the founder as we would share about the faithfulness of Christ and opportunities to minister at home and abroad. The director and his wife became friends of mine, and they were blessed to live in a beautiful five-bedroom home nestled in the mountains in a secluded area of the property. The home was rent-free and available to them to use as a part of their financial package. They absolutely loved the ministry and the area. On one of my trips to the retreat, the director came up to me with a look of excitement on his face I had never seen. He and his wife had both just read a book about the unreached people groups in the world. The book stressed how much time, energy, and money went into repeatedly evangelizing and training people in the same geographical locations. The book emphasized that even in this period of world history there is a vast number who have never been reached with the gospel. The Lord pierced both of their hearts with a burden to become trained and to find a mission group that they could work with together to help share the gospel with these unreached individuals. Their heart was to fulfill the great commission and to take the gospel to the whole world. I pondered within myself how difficult it must be to even think about leaving this beautiful area with a large rent-free home for your family and to so radically change your lives. Beyond that, they would have to raise every dollar to provide for their needs while on the mission field. This would mean literally living by faith for the rest of their lives. It was a beautiful transition to watch as this couple jointly surrendered their hearts to the call and purpose of the Lord. I'm pleased to say that I have watched their faithfulness on the field for over 40 years, with many of those years being in a leadership position and training many other young couples to carry this torch to a new generation.

I can imagine some of you are thinking, *I'm not going to begin to pray about my spouse and myself serving in some capacity because God may speak to us about going overseas!* While that scenario is rare, it does occasionally happen. I would encourage you to relax knowing that when God does call a couple to take those extreme measures, He will, in His wisdom, place the vision in both of your hearts. Some couples may even find themselves testing the waters and realizing that there are different methods and opportunities to support missions that are better suited to them without being in a foreign field. In fact, couples who feel called to foreign missions may never leave their hometown. Numerous opportunities and supportive roles are available to aid those serving around the world. In situations where only one spouse feels called to the mission field, one option could be serving on short-term mission trips while the other spouse can provide support by accepting the responsibilities for the family and home for that short but important season. Home or abroad, it is still an important ministry in the sight of the Lord.

That was the case in my life. In September 1975 I was in a special season of spiritual growth and hunger. I was praying about the calling that I had begun to sense in my heart and how the Lord may want to use my life. Since age 12, my goal has been to work in the automobile industry in some way. I absolutely loved cars from an early age and began to work long hours as a teenager to purchase my first sports car. At this particular season of my life, I began working with my father-in-law, a wonderful Christian man whom I loved dearly. He had begun a successful pre-owned car dealership. My dream was about to become a reality as we planned our future together. However, as my spiritual hunger increased so did my time in prayer. I also began to read scriptures about fasting and how the Holy Spirit could use this self-sacrifice to help us become more focused on His voice and plan for our lives. My life was deeply impacted by His word and prolonged times in prayer.

It certainly wasn't a normal occurrence for me! However, I was deep in prayer one evening after work and I saw what looked to me like a framed picture. In the picture, I saw Christ, as the Lamb of God sacrificing himself for my sins. No, I did not see his face, but at that moment, I knew that it was Him. The point being, He reminded me that His grace was sufficient for me and that through faith, not only were my sins forgiven but that He could use someone like me to share the gospel with others. Next, I saw countless individuals with darker skin than me worshiping God.

At that very moment, I knew in my heart that the day would come when I would be somewhere overseas preaching the good news of Christ to many people.

It wasn't very long after that that I began preaching in various venues and eventually established a new church. Less than three years later, I read a book by an individual from Africa that set my heart ablaze. I contacted the author and asked him to come and preach at the church I was pastoring the next time he was in our country. He was kind enough to accept the invitation. At the end of three days, when it was time for him to leave, he looked at me and said, "My son is going to India in two weeks to preach in a huge crusade, and you are going with him." I had no money or passport. Miraculously, God provided the money for the trip, and I flew to Washington DC and got a one-day passport service. Two weeks later, I met his son and 11 other team members in the Air India terminal at JFK airport. I didn't know any of them, but I knew God had ordained this season of ministry for me long ago and I was more than enthusiastic to join the team. The lead evangelist tried to prepare me for what I would soon experience. On the opening night of the crusade, approximately 40,000 people attended. The following night it was estimated that nearly 75,000 gathered. On numerous trips together, we were blessed to minister to 150,000 – 200,000 people in a single service, according to local estimates.

I continued to go back, taking others with me, and working in various small villages preaching, baptizing new converts, and supporting local pastors. Now, as exciting as all of this was for me, my wife did not sense a calling in her heart to go on these trips. We used to laugh about the fact that I probably told her too many stories about the many lizards in our motel rooms or encounters with cobra snakes or rats in our restaurants. That was not always the case, of course, as I met some of the most wonderful people who were gracious, kind, and supportive in extremely clean homes. Nevertheless, the reality was we were not always staying in wonderful facilities when we traveled.

I tell you that story that I may share this with you - I could not have accomplished any of those things without the support of my wife. There was never one trip that she discouraged me from going. At no time did she argue with me or make me feel guilty about the fact that my absence would be placing a much greater burden and responsibility on her to take care of our three children while working outside of the home. She always helped make sure the clothes I needed were clean and packed. She worked out the schedule to make sure all of the children were at school and on time for additional activities from art to ball practice.

We all have individual gifts as couples, but the calling is that we should always support one another whether it is on a mission field or in your local church.

Approximately 18 years ago our church was in transition. Our founding pastor, Dr. Charles Brown had retired, and our eldership was prayerfully considering who would be our next senior pastor. Though some thought with my years of experience I would be asked to take that position, the eldership all felt that our former youth pastor, Mike Devine was to fill the role. They certainly made the right decision. The church has prospered and grown in numerous ways under Pastor Mike's leadership.

Dr. Gary Chapman, the author of "The Five Love Languages", whom I consider a dear friend and mentor, discussed this season of transition with me. In his wisdom he asked me this question, "Do you feel the need and call to be a senior pastor?" He continued by commenting that if I felt that specific calling at my age, I should go ahead and pursue that position, even if it was somewhere else. I was serving as a Family Life Pastor and thoroughly enjoyed the aspects of counseling and ministering to individuals and families at our church. Brother Gary encouraged me to pray about a new outlet to use my gifts more fully. After prayer and consideration, I felt I was to stay at the church and continue to serve in my current role. However, I felt led to start a new ministry within the church to teach couples the fundamentals of a godly marriage and how to obtain loving, fulfilling relationships that most people only dream of. We started a class called "Love's Journey". In the beginning, I asked several couples to support the class in numerous ways. Members of this leadership team would help reach out to new couples to tell them about the class and its benefits. They provided a light breakfast each Sunday as many of the young moms and dads had little time to eat, especially as they were getting their children ready to come to church. They helped by planning activities outside of the church with numerous day trips as well as weekend marriage seminars. Each one of those couples served faithfully and was of tremendous help. However, here we are 18 years later and one of the couples is still extremely instrumental in the success of the class. Mike and Stephanie. The two of them, as a team, have sacrificed tremendously doing everything from sending out cards, planning meals, shopping, decorating for banquets, and preparing large meals for various events.

Over the years we have had banquets where hundreds attended which were provided free of charge to area pastors and their spouses, area law enforcement officers, first responders, and others as an evening to inspire and encourage them individually and in their marriages.

When I initially asked Mike and Stephanie to help, they probably wondered why I was asking them. Quite simply, I saw a potential in them to be a great resource and blessing to the class and my experience assured me that they would be greatly blessed for their efforts. I had prayed there would be a willingness in their hearts as well, and there certainly was! Like every couple who serves, they have to find a balance between their work, family responsibilities, extracurricular activities, and service at church. As Stephanie seemingly has unlimited energy and zeal, Mike grinned and said, "Sometimes I have to rein her in." Soon we were all grinning knowing that was the truth. They both are very willing to serve others but when there is a need, it almost draws Stephanie like a magnet to help.

Mike especially was motivated to help and serve, having watched an older couple in the church serving in many different capacities over the years. He continued to notice this gentleman's willingness to roll his sleeves up and get involved. That became a great wake-up moment in knowing that he both could and should find ways to serve and be a blessing to others himself.

We should all be aware that when we are doing the right thing and blessing others, it is a great motivation and encouragement to other people. Oftentimes, those individuals do not even know they are being used to encourage others. They are just doing what God has placed in their heart as a means of honoring him and blessing His kingdom.

Stephanie's willingness to serve has had her involved in everything from our Love's Journey class to the children's choir. She has served with extraordinary joy and enthusiasm for years. I believe this is where God's wisdom within the marriage works so well. Mike has seen times when Stephanie's love for the Lord and heart to help others could bring her nearly to a place of exhaustion. Wisely, he has encouraged her to reevaluate her service in different seasons so that she can fully use her gifts and yet reserve time and energy for her family and herself.

Conversely, Stephanie helps balance Mike by helping him to see ongoing needs, such as we have within the class and beyond as he focuses on his career and other responsibilities. This special couple serves many people within the church but also within their neighborhood and community. It brings them great joy and deep contentment to be able to do this. However, one of the most wonderful things is that it has allowed them to serve together in many different capacities which has continued to enrich their marriage and relationship, as well as inspire other couples to pick up the torch and do the same thing.

Lastly, I want to mention Rick and Deirdre, a couple that we have been blessed to know these last few years. As a couple, Rick and Deirdre both were determined to learn more about God's plan for the Christian marriage and home. Both had been involved in previous relationships and understood the great joys of committed relationships as well as the heartaches that we sometimes experience when relationships fail. Now, as a blended family that includes Deirdre's children, they also wanted to make sure that they set the example that they should for the children.

As a couple, they were just trying to find ways to become more involved in the church and continue to learn and grow in their knowledge of God's word and His purpose for their lives. However, when offered the opportunity through a well-known children's evangelist to join his team on an inner-city mission trip to Buffalo, New York, they felt as though they should at least consider it. Prior to this, Rick had been involved in helping to lead a ministry for the young boys within the church. Truthfully, he had simply planned to assist with that but soon found himself in a leadership role. For them, it seemed as though these opportunities to serve were coming quickly. At times, it almost seemed too quickly but the Lord prepared them both for each step of the way. Once again, we see the truth that if God calls someone to do a task, He will equip them. Often, the willingness of someone's heart to serve is equally important to, or even more important than, a particular skill set they may possess.

After praying and discussing it, they decided to take their two sons on the mission trip. They fed the hungry, encouraged those who were down and out and helped in various levels of street ministry to those in the neighborhood. You may think you would feel awkward in doing that, well you're not alone. This couple was certainly pulled way out of their comfort zone just as countless other couples have been.

This trip ended up being life-changing for the entire family and thus far has led to additional domestic mission trips in the north and southwest as well as continued service in their local church. Even as I write this, I learned that this couple just returned from a trip to Alaska with a group from our church, supporting the wonderful work of Samaritan's Purse.

However, this special couple did not see these opportunities on their horizon, much less the incredible life lessons to be learned and the deep fulfillment in helping so many others. The deep blessings in this mom and dad's hearts as well as the seed that has been sown in their young sons all began with a willingness to make themselves available for God's service.

I could convey to you many stories and testimonies of individuals and couples just like yourself who have realized the Lord's wonderful and personal plan that He designed for them and through them as they acknowledged His sovereignty and how it includes each one of us as His children.

Have you and your spouse found an opportunity that would allow the two of you to serve others together? If not, I encourage you to begin looking today and praying for direction. I have no doubt the Lord will show you a way that you can serve together which will both strengthen your marriage and be a blessing to others.

Part II ~ The Importance of Emotional Intimacy

Chapter 8: *Searching For Personal Oneness*

We are all searching for oneness with the person we love.

O magnify the Lord with me, let us exalt his name together. Psalm 34:3

It was a day just like any other day. Then Jared walked into the house and looked at Tina as she was preparing dinner, she noticed that he had the biggest smile on his face she had ever seen as he happily announced, "Pack your bags for our dream trip! I received an unexpected bonus today!"

Before she allowed herself to get too excited, she looked him square in the eyes and asked skeptically, "Are you kidding me? Please don't kid me about this." Jared was still smiling ear to ear, "No, I am serious! Let's set a date and book our flight and accommodations!" Tina jumped up and down in the kitchen like a child at Christmas.

This young couple were good stewards of their money. They had been saving for over two years for this exciting ski vacation, and the bonus put them over the budgeted amount needed for the trip.

Both looked forward to the trip, but especially Tina. They had attended and met each other at a university in the mountains of North Carolina. They had spent much of their free time skiing at Beech Mountain and Sugar Mountain during the winter months, two of North Carolina's most popular ski slopes. Snow skiing was Tina's favorite sport and she had dreamed of skiing some of the legendary Colorado slopes for years. She often thought, *If I had the money, where would I go? Vail, Keystone, Beavercreek, Crested Butte, maybe Breckenridge?*

She had a drawer full of brochures and catalogs describing many of the area's top skiing destinations. She would occasionally review the various slope sizes and conditions as well as the beautiful and inviting chalets and numerous recommended accommodations, and now all of her daydreaming was about to become a reality.

Soon, the day came, and they flew to Colorado for an entire week on their dream vacation. Once they arrived, they settled into their beautiful chalet. It was everything she had ever dreamed it would be. They wasted no time in hitting the slopes. Their adrenaline was flowing, and love was in the air! The next morning, they left for a full day on the slopes, expecting to relax and get away from the pressures of work and life. It was an unbelievable day. That evening they were enjoying a delicious dinner and the warmth of the crackling fire in the beautiful rock fireplace near their table. As they sat discussing the beauty of the slopes as well as their challenges, they heard familiar voices. It was Greg and Cindy, friends and dorm mates from college. What were the chances of them meeting here like this? They had moved away several years ago.

They were thrilled to see each other and quickly decided to spend the next day skiing together. They all had a wonderful day together and it seemed like an exciting double-date experience. They had a lot to catch up on and decided to eat dinner together that night. For the next two days and the following morning, the two couples were inseparable. Then it was time for Greg and Cindy to fly home. After they departed, Jared and Tina spent the afternoon skiing by themselves, which provided a time of solitude. Tina felt so grateful to be there as well as happy to have seen her friends, but she was having some troubling thoughts. Some of the conversations that the two couples had shared while talking and enjoying their meals together left Tina wondering if her two friends understood her better than her own husband did. They made comments about her thoughts and feelings that were foreign to Jared. She also began to think back on the weeks before their trip, she had been feeling unappreciated and sometimes misunderstood. As Jared had gotten so busy in his own world with work and his friends, there were times she felt very much alone. She didn't want to ruin the rest of the trip, but she knew that once they got home, there were some things that she and Jared were going to need to discuss.

The trip was wonderful, and she genuinely appreciated it, but then again, Jared loved snow skiing almost as much as she did. She thought about how clueless Jared was to some of their friend's observations about Tina's comments and preferences. She also thought about some of the unnecessary comments Jared made during the trip about how cute other women were, even though he always said he was just kidding about it, or how critical he was of her when she lost her balance. She could not remember one time that he had commented about her being cute during the entire trip, and had he even told her once that he loved her?

As special as the trip was, she had to face a grim reality, they had drifted apart. Were they still best friends? Besides skiing and the trip, did they still share the same interests and values in life anymore? She was not looking for things to start an argument, but the more she thought about their relationship, the more warning signs she began to see. She knew that as soon as she started the conversation with him involving her concern, they didn't share the same deep level of intimacy they once had, he would comment about how great their sex life was.

But was it? Maybe for him, it was, but did he even care if it was as enjoyable for her? Thoughts were racing in her mind. He just wanted time for sex, but she needed a reason for it. Was she that different from most other women? Regardless of how others felt, she needed both an emotional attachment and loving support from him first. Tina was correct in her assessment, however, that was only the tip of the iceberg and an indicator of deeper issues that were going on within the relationship. Though this couple was still in love, they had much to learn about the benefits and joy of a deeper level of emotional intimacy.

As of the time of this writing, I have 50 years of marital experience. I was married to Suzette, my teenage sweetheart, for almost 43 years before the Lord called her to heaven after a valiant three-year battle with ALS. We spent decades being taught, studying, and discussing what it meant to us to feel close and deeply loved. We were truly best friends who were deeply in love with one another, and we never stopped trying to learn how to share our hearts and dreams in deeper and more meaningful ways with one another.

Since her homegoing, as I mentioned, I remarried. Vickie, who is also widowed after more than 40 years to her loving and hard-working husband, an absolute warrior who battled kidney disease and cancer before his homegoing. Jerry was the closest of friends to me, who I loved like a brother. Their deaths were only weeks apart. Vickie and I would have never dreamed, even in a thousand years, that we would eventually feel led to be married and spend the rest of our lives together. Most everyone was very happy for us. Some were surprised, but the two of us were shocked. However, God had a master plan that allowed two friends to get to know each other in a completely different and deeper level. Marriage based on the truths of God's word, openness, honesty, and trust are always wonderful. Love grows out of that environment every time.

In almost as many years, I have been in the ministry and spoken to couples thousands of times about the deepest issues in their hearts and marriages. In addition, I have led marriage classes and seminars for over 30 years. I trust that I can share some life-changing truths with some who read these pages that will enable you to share life with your best friend in a truly fulfilling relationship.

I can and will share terms and thoughts with you that can help you better understand what emotional intimacy is and what it looks like in marriage. However, the more challenging part will be for you to apply these terms and truths to your mind and heart. Most everyone wants their spouse to change in some way to become more fulfilling and enticing to them. I will suggest to you that the changes must start within yourself. That is not to say that there are not numerous ways that your spouse could become more understanding or loving. But the way that you love them may well make those changes possible or even desirable within your spouse. In addition to that, becoming a less self-centered individual with more of a servant's heart will change your view not only of your spouse but of life in general. This will enable you to become a much more fulfilled and contented individual.

Philippians 2:3 *Do nothing from selfish ambition or conceit, but in humility count others more significant than yourselves.*

Earlier, I referred to a Christian retreat in the mountains of North Carolina founded by my good friend, Betty Mottsinger. Numerous times with a smile and a laugh, she would comment on the fact that the Lord would send young couples from the surrounding area to her for marriage counseling. But Betty was never married! She had fully committed her life to the Lord. At first, she wondered what she could possibly tell any couple that would have an impact on their marriage when she had never been married for a single day herself. Without question, the Lord gave her two truths that she told many couples, and I have shared many, times because of its validity.

First, she would refer to the Scripture found in Genesis 2:24, which says, *"Now a man shall leave his father and mother and be joined to his wife, and they shall become one flesh."*

Betty would paraphrase the passage by saying this: "When you leave, you cleave." In other words, when you commit to loving someone in the covenant of marriage, make up your mind that it is for life. Quit looking for loopholes and ways to get out of it. Find a way to both honor God and honor your spouse as you work out your differences.

Secondly, she would say, *"Learn to love your husband or wife the way they are, not the way you want them to be."*

She was instructing the couples to quit comparing their husband or wife to countless others and picking and choosing different character traits that they now wish they had. Love them just the way they are, just as the Lord loves them. Besides, the Lord loves you just the way that you are, as well.

I would grin and tell that sweet sister that the Lord had given her two powerful truths that could transform any marriage, if only they would listen. Will you listen? Are you listening to the loving truths of God's word instead of the voices of disappointment and frustration in your mind and heart that you have allowed to grow inside of you? Voices that have diminished your acts of kindness and commitment to your marriage?

Now, I encourage you to decide once and for all that you will never settle, not one more day of your married life, for mediocrity. Regardless of the emotional intimacy or lack of it in your marriage today, the Lord has without question created the marriage relationship between a husband and wife to be a reflection of His love for His church which is His bride.

Interestingly, in Ephesians 5:25, husbands are instructed to love their wives just like Christ loved the church and gave Himself for her. Numerous scriptures could be used, but the biblical truth here instructs husbands and wives to wholly and completely give their lives to love and support one another, just as Christ gave His life for us.

Happiness is not the highest calling within a marriage.

The highest calling and responsibility for every husband and wife is to surrender their heart and life to the Lord, their Creator. To find His plan and purpose for their life and to walk it out daily and when married, to help their spouse both understand and walk in God's will and purpose for their life. That is true success. That is eternal success. Ambitions less than this are temporary and will fade with time.

Chapter 9: *Understanding Emotional Intimacy*

We have more to learn about the one we love.

The following definition gives a general understanding of emotional intimacy. However, our goal is to come to an understanding of truly deep and practical emotional intimacy that can bring the deepest levels of love and friendship to your marriage.

Emotional intimacy involves a perception of closeness to another that allows the sharing of personal feelings, accompanied by expectations of understanding, affirmation, and demonstration of caring.

No couple has ever walked down the aisle and committed themselves to one another in marriage with the hopes of living a life dominated by anger, frustration, misunderstandings, and rejection. On the contrary, we all get married not only dreaming of but expecting a life filled with harmony and support. Emotional intimacy begins with a couple experiencing a general sense of oneness and love.

Scripture calls a husband and wife to "oneness" in heart, but that does not mean "sameness". The Lord has deposited and created particular gifts and strengths within both the husband and wife. They are to be used to complete and balance the other. Walking in the greatest depths of tender love and emotional intimacy will not come by trying to force your husband or wife to be like you. As you develop your relationship with Christ and become more like Him, and you encourage your spouse to become more like Him, you will automatically become closer together because you both will have more of His traits. You will be more loving, forgiving, patient, etc... The Lord does not shy away from terms of intimacy. He created all intimacy whether it be spiritual, emotional, or physical. Christ teaches us how to be close to him by the way that He loves us and becomes close to us. We love him because He first loved us. Learn from His example, and let love begin in you.

"Jesus told his disciples, anyone who wants to be first must be the very last, and the servant of all." Mark 9:35

"The Son of Man did not come to be served, but to serve, and to give his life a ransom (or for the deliverance of) for many." Matthew 20:28

So at the core of developing emotional intimacy, we must learn to place our focus on our husband or wife. Make it your life mission to understand them, to serve them within healthy boundaries and biblical guidelines, to bring fulfillment to their heart and lives, as well as to motivate them into a deeper pursuit to more fully know and represent Christ in their generation.

Regardless, of how well you believe you know your spouse, there are always deeper levels of insight we can obtain to draw closer together. In the busyness of life, whether it involves work and maintaining a home and vehicles or additional responsibilities in raising and taking care of children, we seldom take the time to focus on getting to know one another better. It takes both dedicated time and intentional effort to get to know one another at a deeper level. There is no substitute for either.

Why not start here?

List three things that your spouse does that are very meaningful to you and make you feel loved and appreciated.

_____
_____
_____
_____
_____

List three things that you would appreciate if your spouse began to do that you believe could help the two of you become closer.

_____
_____
_____
_____
_____

List three things that your spouse would say are the most meaningful and loving things you do for them.

_____
_____
_____
_____
_____
_____

List three things that you believe your spouse would appreciate you beginning to do for them to make them feel more loved and appreciated.

_____
_____
_____
_____
_____
_____

The wise husband and wife will always make an effort to know the true thoughts and feelings of one another. And honestly, sometimes their priorities change during the different seasons of life, just like yours do. Are you sure you know what they would put on their list at this time? To ignore the deep issues, concerns, and feelings of their hearts is both selfish and hardhearted. You're sabotaging your own relationship and will eventually get the opposite effects from your marriage of what you want and need yourself.

Emotional intimacy can have many building blocks. Truthful and respectful conversation, a much-appreciated friendship and companionship like no other, feelings of sometimes indescribable closeness, and openness and vulnerability that allow for uninhibited love and unquestioned trust. The couple enjoying emotional intimacy finds themselves relaxed and comfortable in one another's conversations as well as in each other's arms. The couple enjoying emotional intimacy is a couple who appreciates laughter, not at one another, but with one another. They truly understand freedom and devotion to one another. A couple with mature emotional intimacy is a couple who lives with an attitude of forgiveness and selflessness toward one another. They support and believe in one another even if they do not fully understand each other in a particular moment of decision-making or processing.

The couple who truly comprehends emotional intimacy is committed to the deepest levels of ongoing friendship with the one who can share their deepest dreams without fear of ridicule. They know their closest friend and lover has their back and will always lift up their heart and hands in support and encouragement. They live with an attitude of sincere gratefulness and appreciation for each other.

Let's face it, with these observations being made, most couples have their work cut out for them. You may as well. If so, let's get started now.

I believe the best place to start is a better understanding of how you communicate with one another. It doesn't matter if you are concerned about your future, parenting issues, or finances. Every step toward oneness must flow through your conversations.

Do you consider yourself a good conversationalist? Would your spouse agree with your personal observation? I lost count long ago of how many couples have sat in front of me discussing their frustrations about feeling misunderstood. While in sincere conversations, husbands have looked at me and stated, "I know that talking about things is important to her, and I think that I am trying and really do a good job." Even before he finishes his statement, tears are beginning to pour out of his wife's eyes, tears that are saying, *he does not have a clue how to communicate with me or what I need from him.*

On the other hand, wives who consider themselves to be good communicators with an air of self-approval have told me that they are always willing to talk to their husbands about their issues and even wish that they would talk to her more often. Many times, this is when I've seen the husbands turn around to look at their wives with an expression ranging from frustration to anger. *No, you don't talk to me. You belittle me and talk down to me, like I'm in middle school. If I don't agree with everything you, say you, are disrespectful and withdraw from me, sometimes for days. How am I supposed to be able to share my heart with you when you judge and ridicule every word that comes out of my mouth? That makes me want to just keep it to myself and forget it.*

Many men admittedly find it normal and even prefer to speak fewer words and give their nod or simple verbal response, instead of a lengthy conversation with their wives. Additionally, numerous husbands find lengthy conversations unnecessary and repetitive. His wife, however, often continues to bring up some of the same topics creating tension in the relationship. While it may be true that the wife could rethink the way she is presenting herself and her questions, I often tell this frustrated husband that his wife simply wants and needs to make a point to him that he has not yet understood. No wife wants to be a source of frustration to her husband. Normally she is repeating the same conversation in an attempt to simply say, "Why don't you understand me?" Or possibly, "Why don't you care about how this situation is affecting me and making me feel?" Husbands especially need to understand that the "ability to listen" is one of the most important components of good communication.

Many needed conversations are shut down before they begin with sarcastic glares and rude gestures. You can work through your deepest frustrations and disappointments with one another when you take the following approach:

First, look at your spouse through the eyes of the Lord. They are created in His image and His likeness. He never made any mistakes. Acknowledge that your spouse deserves to be respected, even if their attitude does not reflect that of an individual who is conducting themselves in a proper manner. His intent is always to bless and enrich their life and understanding. Yours should be, also.

Secondly, do your best to look at the situation at hand through your spouse's eyes, not yours. Our past experiences influence us all, and it is possible that even though you have been married for some time, you do not fully understand the deepest needs, concerns, and fears that are deep in your wife's or your husband's minds and hearts. Sometimes, it is extremely challenging and difficult for someone to reach into the deepest recesses of their soul to share information that few people if anyone, know about.

I am going to make a confession here for the sake of an example. Vic and I had been married for approximately six years. On a beautiful summer day, I was enjoying the sunshine and working on some projects in my shop. There was a lot that I wanted and needed to accomplish that day, and admittedly, I was in high gear. My shop is a detached garage approximately 30 feet from the house sharing the same driveway. I would eventually be back and forth from the house to the shop numerous times that day. We are 100 feet off the highway, it was in broad daylight and as I stated, the shop is only 30 feet from the house. I hurried from the shop to the house to pick up something and the storm door was locked. I didn't understand that at all. I rang the doorbell, and my wife let me in, and I picked up the item I needed in the house. I went straight back to work on my projects and got absorbed in what I was doing. Soon it was time to eat, so I went back to the house. The door was locked again. How frustrating! I grabbed the door and pulled on it to open it quickly to run into the house. Once again, I rang the doorbell and waited for her to come unlock the door. I'm thinking, *will you please hurry?* Vic unlocked the door, and I went into the house...finally. I relaxed, ate something, and went back out to the shop to finish the project. Forgetting what had happened earlier because of my enjoyment in the day, I walked back to the house later in the day, grabbed the door handle to pull on it, and I was locked out again. Without even thinking, I slapped the doorframe with my hand. That is unusual for me. My family and friends know I rarely get upset. My wife heard me slap the door casing and came to the door and apologized for the door being locked. She could not help but notice the frustration in my voice as I said, "I don't understand why you're locking the door in the middle of the day. I'm only 30 feet away." I could tell that her feelings were hurt by my tone and that she thought she had disappointed me as we live every day to the fullest and we both strive to live with hearts of respect toward one another. First, I apologized to her for hurting her feelings. Secondly, I asked her why she had kept locking the door and told her I simply didn't understand.

The tone of her voice and her body language also let me know that she had no intention of locking the door to frustrate me. She shared with me the story of being a young girl at home with her mom. A man came to their home and beat on the door for some time, trying to break in before her dad, who was a state patrolman, could arrive at the house and confirm that the man had left and that they were safe and secure. It was a terrifying event as they screamed at him they had to get to the one telephone in the house to call for help. They knew the door could swing open any minute from his constant beating on the door. That trauma from decades before, unfortunately, still affected her heart and mind. To this day, I do not see the need at all for that door to be locked when I'm so close by, but I will never again become frustrated with her for doing it or say or do anything at all to make her feel belittled about locking the door behind me. At the same time, I continue to pray that the Lord will heal her heart and take away that memory and fear as one more step of God's healing grace in her life.

We must acknowledge that communication is not just simply about sharing words.

Healthy communication conveys a truthful insight, consisting of both content and meaning.

I will also use the previous misunderstanding as an example of communication.

I had shared my frustration. Vic spoke back clearly with elements of concern and hurt for frustrating me. At the deepest level, unconsciously, she may even have been experiencing a concern within herself that she had never worked through this old fear. The thought may have crossed her mind that an issue in her past had become a problem in our present life, and that wasn't fair. But truly, this happens on a daily basis. A husband is short and derogatory in his comments to his wife and her mind instantly reverts to 20 years ago to a former husband or boyfriend who was very critical of her. Immediately she becomes defensive. Or, possibly, a husband may feel like his wife has nothing to say to him except for one complaint after another. This may trigger unpleasant memories of a voice of disrespect from a past relationship that quickly pushes his buttons and causes him to become angry. Often a wife or husband responds in a moment of conversation with an attitude or response that is far beyond what is necessary or expected. The comment comes across like an attitude on steroids. Husbands and wives are often left speechless, angry, or so frustrated they don't know how to respond.

In the moment we don't always fully understand why we either speak or respond exactly as we do. That day my wife's body language spoke volumes to me, and my body language spoke clearly to her. She was apologetic, but also hurt by my tone. I was frustrated and though I would never yell at her, I was certainly louder and speaking more firmly than I normally do.

Some time ago, Dr. David Olson, founder of Life Innovations, led a national survey of 21,501 married couples in an attempt to identify specific communication issues that are problematic for married couples. Five problems are listed with the corresponding percentage of couples experiencing that problem.

1. I wish my partner were more willing to share feelings 82%
2. I have difficulty asking my partner for what I want   75%
3. my partner does not understand how I feel 72%
4. my partner often refuses to discuss issues/problems 71%
5. my partner makes comments that put me down 67%

I find these numbers staggering. The facts confirm what some cry about, and others joke about surrounding the challenge of understanding one's spouse. Essentially, most husbands and wives are not communicating with each other in a healthy and meaningful manner. Additionally, my concern is that the cycles continue for years and years as couples use the same styles and attitudes during their conversations. The argument normally says, *if you would only change then maybe we can have a productive conversation without arguing or hurting each other.* Too few married adults are willing to look in the mirror and ask themselves what they need to change to help improve communication and emotional intimacy in their relationship. I wish that individuals could understand that being humble does not make you a doormat and that being forgiving does not make you weak. On the contrary, they are both qualities of Christ. Rest assured, His character does not reflect weakness, and neither will yours when you follow in His footsteps.

Countless couples who have divorced have later said that they never could communicate well with their former spouse. Their attempts would end with arguments, insults, or their spouse walking away and not finishing the conversation.

You can learn how to be a good communicator with your spouse.

I often say that in building the marriage and home that we all want and need, we need the correct tools in our toolbox. Communication is as basic in a marital toolbox as a hammer or screwdriver is in your toolbox at home for basic repairs.

Take a moment to do an honest evaluation of how well you communicate. It may not be as good as you think it is.

1. Do you encourage your spouse to share their true thoughts and feelings in an open and safe environment?
2. When you ask them to share, are you doing so with sarcasm in your voice or offensive body language?
3. When they do respond in conversation, are you already forming an opinion or rebuttal before they finish their thoughts?
4. Is your response short, insulting, or close-minded?

5. Do you find yourself needing to be right or getting the last word?

6. Do you find yourself folding your arms or turning your head to look the other way because you disagree or don't like what is being said instead of encouraging your spouse to fully share their thoughts and feelings?

Mutual respect is one of the most important aspects of any healthy relationship and certainly is vital as you learn to expand your skill set in good communication.

As we consider different styles of communication and how to be more effective, let's consider three common styles of communication Dr. Olsen shares that are used in homes countless times a day.

Aggressive communication - This style of communication is used by the individual who is absolutely determined to get their point across. The aggressive communicator often feels that their opinion is superior to the one they are speaking to. Possibly, this individual has felt put down in the past, and they are utterly determined it will not happen again, or they are simply self-centered. *You will hear what I have to say!* This style of communication is disrespectful and nonproductive. Speaking in this manner isolates the speaker and creates a greater separation in the relationship due to the disrespectful and hurtful words and tone.

Passive communication - This individual has as many thoughts or feelings as anyone else but is reluctant to share them. They may think it is better to avoid a spirited exchange (within healthy boundaries) than to have a disagreement. They fail to see the fact that disagreeing is normal and, in truth, can create the opportunity for a couple to both express themselves and learn more about each other as well as their own hearts. A passive communicator could possibly be someone who has been shut down too many times in the past and is not willing to risk being hurt again. Ridicule from the past can cause this individual to feel as though their opinion is not important and to second-guess their self-worth.

Assertive communication - This is the healthiest style of communication, as it allows both parties to fully and completely share their thoughts and hearts in a safe environment. Being assertive is not being aggressive and pushing thoughts down someone else's throat. It simply states, the fact that we are both equal and should speak about the issues that are important to us and the relationship from our personal perspective. Assertive communication allows both the husband and wife to feel valued and understood. It is respectful and productive.

Because of the understanding, support, and validation assertive communication provides, it also encourages continued conversations that bring even more insight and depth to the relationship.

A gentle answer deflects anger, but harsh words make tempers flare. Proverbs 15:1

When I reflect on the different styles of communication, I cannot help but think about numerous couples I have known over the years that have remained locked into unproductive styles of communication. However, there are those exceptions that are very gratifying. Such a transformation came into the lives and hearts of Cain and Melissa. Sometimes things get worse before they get better, and this is a great reminder for anyone reading this to never give up. Continue to pray over your marriage and the way the two of you communicate. Make what changes you can in your own life, and never lose hope.

Cain and Melissa were in their late 30s and were as happy as most any couple you had ever met. The two of them had met at a high school football game. He played football for his school in a larger nearby city. Melissa was a cheerleader for her school in a more rural area about 30 miles away. Call it fate or the will of the Lord, but the two of them crossed paths as mutual friends were hanging out talking to one another in the school parking lot after the game. The two of them hit it off immediately, and though there were no phone numbers exchanged that night, it did not take Cain very long to get back with a mutual friend and get her contact information. Once they began talking, there was no looking back. Sometimes, opposites attract, and it was one of the most exciting experiences of their life.

He enjoyed playing football just like his older brother and his dad did. You could say he was groomed to keep the family tradition alive. He knew he would not play beyond high school, and he kept his commitment to football in the context of his other interests. He was a bright student, and unlike some of his fellow teammates, he enjoyed studying and learning. He was determined to be a success in life, and he dreamed big. Possibly the example he had seen from his self-employed dad had an impact on his life. He had always seen his dad work long and hard hours and he appreciated the benefits of his dad's success. At that age and mindset, he overlooked the disappointments and loneliness his mom dealt with as she took a backseat to the family business. His mom was extremely grateful for all her hard-working husband had provided, but there were times she just needed him to slow down and spend time with her.

Cain and Melissa continued dating and got married the year after Cain graduated college.

Melissa had obtained a two-year degree herself and then went to work in her uncle's gardening and landscaping store. She worked 25 hours a week. She loved working there as it allowed the social butterfly to meet new people as well as take care of their regular friends and customers on an ongoing basis. Besides, she was an outdoor girl. Melissa grew up experiencing an enjoyable childhood which included growing up on 30 acres of land that included pastureland, beautiful woods, and a large pond. She felt like this was the dream home and property that everyone should want.

Cain always enjoyed being at her home when he would go to see her. He saw it as a relaxing place to hang out but never had a desire to keep up with that much property. However, he had no idea how much that lifestyle had impacted Melissa. It was her safe haven. A place where she could enjoy riding their horses or simply taking walks around the pond to just think and be creative, or even cry when she would go through challenging and hurtful times as a teenager. She enjoyed everything about their garden: planting the seeds, watching all of the vegetables and flowers grow, and joining her mom and her grandmother in the kitchen when it came time for canning and freezing the harvest.

After the young couple were married, they stayed in the area as Cain had been hired by a national company with a branch in his hometown. He worked long and hard and upper management took notice. Melissa was always very proud of him and supportive when he would come home and tell her of a compliment he had received from his boss or an increase in his pay or position. Besides, the long hours that Cain worked allowed her free time to enjoy the spacious and inviting farm life she had always enjoyed. Though Melissa enjoyed every minute with her family and time on the farm, she did not allow it to interfere with her marriage. She wanted to be the best wife ever. Melissa kept her house very clean, and Cain was always fortunate to come home to an orderly home. She had no problems having a meal ready for Cain when he got home but oftentimes, they enjoyed that time in the kitchen together preparing the evening meal. The balance between married life and enjoying the life she had always known was so idyllic that Melissa would have been happy to have enjoyed her entire life just as things were.

The only thing that had changed negatively was the fact that Cain had become much more inconsiderate in the way that he spoke to Melissa. At times, he would be sharp with his words, and his attitude would be cold and inconsiderate. Sometimes it troubled her, but she tried not to worry about it too much. Besides, the few times that she tried to talk to Cain about it he would get loud and defensive and say things that deeply hurt her. Sometimes, his words brought her to tears, but that did not seem to concern him very much either.

Then the day came that she had dreaded but sometimes thought may happen. Her hard-working, goal-oriented husband had been offered a promotion in the corporate headquarters. This would mean not only moving over 500 miles away but she would also be living in a city for the first time in her life. With little to no thought about how Melissa would feel or be affected, Cain had accepted the new position without even discussing it with her, only to come home and announce the fact that they were moving. He incorrectly assumed Melissa would be as excited about the news as he was. Before she could even explain to him how proud she was of him and that she was content with their current income and lifestyle, he loudly interrupted her. He told her that they were moving and that she should be grateful for his hard work that had been rewarded, and that they would have an opportunity to enjoy the finer things in life. Cain's aggressive style of communication began the erosion of the couple's emotional intimacy far more than he could have imagined.

At this point, it was evident that the stress and anxiety that had built up in Cain the past couple of years since he set his personal goal of obtaining this job, coupled with his definition of the finer things in life, had taken a higher priority than Melissa's desires or feelings. She was hurt and devastated but had always wanted to be a supportive and loving wife. She hated the thought of leaving her family behind and her connection to the farm. As for all her friends at church and work, she was heartbroken to think that she would be leaving them as well. She was simply a small-town girl who was fully content.

However, she read between the lines of Cain's self-centered announcement about moving. She wasn't sure how he meant it, but she knew what she heard. She heard him say, "Pack your bags and come with me whether you want to or not if we are going to be together."

Melissa was not only disappointed at the way that her husband had announced that they would move, but she despised it and the way it left her feeling so hurt. It's as though her feelings and opinion didn't really matter. She honestly felt like he had talked down to her with a disrespectful attitude and tone that she had never heard before. During the next month as they were planning for their move and packing their boxes, she was able to have some good conversations with

Cain about all that had been said and how they could have handled it differently.

It was yet to be seen how his dominating and self-centered decision and announcement would affect their marriage.

Death and life are in the power of the tongue, and those who love it and indulge it will eat its fruit but also bear the consequences of their words Proverbs 18:21

Few lessons in life are as important as learning the power of the words you speak and their effects on others. Speaking words of life and hope into your spouse develops emotional intimacy and a growing oneness.

Cain's new destructive behavior would quite possibly have effects on everything from their sexual intimacy to their spiritual intimacy. Such aggressive tones and behavior often leave a wife feeling disappointed with her husband. It also makes it more challenging for her to see him as the spiritual head of her home that God called to protect her as he exhibits a Christ-like love for her.

It could also be very possible that with this new move comes a greater sense of anxiety in Cain. He had always enjoyed sexual intimacy with his wife, but sometimes consciously or unconsciously, anxiety and stress can cause a husband to find himself both wanting and needing a greater level of relaxing and fulfilling intimacy with his wife. The problem is, with her heart wounded and feeling disrespected, she may find it more challenging to be as available and loving to her husband as she had in the past. I will address this more fully later in the book.

The day finally came when the moving van arrived and began the process of loading all of their belongings. Melissa tearfully gave hugs to her family members and a couple of her closest friends who had come to help that day. Cain gave firm handshakes with a confident smile to those who were there, prepared to embark on his new season of life and conquest. As a part of their financial package, the company was providing an apartment to them for 90 days to allow them to explore the housing market.

The couple found a helpful and understanding agent, but it did not take long for the two of them to realize that even with the additional income it would not allow them to obtain their dream house. It appeared to Melissa that the more homes they looked at the smaller they appeared, and the dream of having even two or 3 acres was quickly removed from any transaction. Eventually, the couple found a home they both liked in a safe and trendy section of town. The home included a lot of less than ½ an acre. Cain's thoughts were, *Great, not as much upkeep which will allow me more free time to play golf on my days off.* Melissa's thoughts were, *I grew up helping tend a garden twice the size of this entire lot.*

In the upcoming days, the couple worked hard to unpack all their boxes and make this new house their home. Of course, Cain was eager to make a good impression and went early and stayed late many evenings as he worked hard to succeed at his new job. The smiles and compliments from those in upper management positions created a constant determination in him to succeed and please them. Clearly, his love language was words of affirmation. Melissa had understood that for some time as the two of them had read Dr. Gary Chapman's book, <u>The Five Love Languages</u>. After reading the book the two of them did the assessment. As clearly as they had learned that his love language was "words of affirmation", the two of them had learned that Melissa's love language was "quality time". The problem was, Cain had evidently forgotten Melissa's love language, or it was so far down his list of priorities it didn't matter.

Though Melissa had made some new friends in both the neighborhood and a local church, her world was still very limited to what she had known her entire life. She missed her family but knew that her place was there with her husband. She loved Cain with her whole heart, and that is where she wanted to be, she just did not expect to be feeling so unhappy and unfulfilled. She had never experienced such emptiness before. She also missed everything about farm life. The peace and serenity of her walks, the animals, and working in the garden.

Six months after they moved, Cain arrived home from work to find Melissa crying again. "Why do you stay so sad?" he asked. "We are so blessed and fortunate." Sometimes she would feel guilty as she realized that was true. However, she was extremely lonely and expected to live out of her element and to be happy about it. The truth was, due to the disrespect and rejection she had been dealing with, she found herself becoming far more passive in her communication with Cain. She had always felt like she could speak her mind without being ridiculed. She knew fully well that everyone was not supposed to agree with her, but at least both people would have an opportunity to express their concerns or even their desires or fears. That was not the case anymore, and she just began to close down and keep most of her thoughts to herself. This always ends up being an unhealthy scenario. In a healthy relationship, both individuals must have an opportunity to freely share their hearts and thoughts in an open and safe environment. Looking at any topic in life from two different aspects is not only normal, but it can also often be very healthy and productive. However, it must be done in an environment based on mutual respect.

That next Saturday, with a big smile on his face, Cain announced, "Get ready, I want to take you somewhere." With both curiosity and excitement, Melissa got ready and got in their car. "Where are we going?" she asked. He told her that he knew this adjustment hadn't been as easy for her as it had for him, and that she was lonely. She found herself feeling very hopeful and excited that he finally understood that she needed more of his time and attention. He played golf almost every weekend with his friends from work. "Networking" he would always say. Soon, she realized where they were headed, they were headed to a dog shelter! *What*?! As though he had figured out how to solve their problem and her needs, he announced his great reveal, "I know you miss the animals on the farm. Let's go inside and you choose a dog. That way you will have the companionship that you've been looking for." *Really*?! She sadly thought, *I could scream at you at the top of my lungs and not speak to you for weeks for not realizing that it is **your** companionship and love that I need.* Melissa simply said, "I cannot believe you", as she sat staring out of the windshield. He wisely quieted down as she processed the moment. They finally went inside and when she saw the animals, she realized how much she had missed the animals on the farm and, well, it would be enjoyable to have a small dog at the house. There in one of the cages, one of the cutest puppies there ever was looked up at her and stole her heart. "Okay", she said, "I'll take that one."

In the upcoming months, Melissa did enjoy the company of her new puppy but continued to deal daily with the disappointment that her husband did not understand her need for more of his love and companionship, as well as the lifestyle that brought peace and fulfillment to her.

With the countless adjustments to be made working a new job and living in a new city, a year passed quickly. It was the most fulfilling year of Cain's life. It was the most unhappy and disappointing year of Melissa's.

Even though it was a year of personal pain and disappointment for Melissa in many ways, there was a part of her heart that felt very satisfied. It was as though, in some sense, she was pleased with herself and that she realized she was growing and maturing as a young woman and as a Christian. Even in her deepest moments of despair, she had tried to deal with them in a manner that wasn't mean and disrespectful to her husband. She had watched other women lash out in their anger and disappointment with their husbands in ways that destroyed their manhood and left them feeling rejected and hopeless. She had seen firsthand that there are times when such a husband never rebounds to a place where he learns to love his wife properly or to truly find himself or his purpose in life. She did not want that. She did try to explain herself as she should have, but she refrained from the screaming and degrading comments that sometimes went through her mind. The two passages in her devotional the week before they moved had served her well. They explained to her that she could walk in a determined faith and that her actions and attitudes would not only bless her husband, but also help him to continue to grow and develop as a man, and especially as a Christ-honoring man.

Yes, Mark 9:35 and Matthew 20:28, two passages about servanthood had changed her outlook forever. She acknowledged that if Christ himself did not come to earth to be served, but to serve others, she should do the same. She knew that this was not an act of weakness but an act of strength, love, and service. With this in mind, even in her disappointment during this first year away from home she did her best to acknowledge

Cain's needs. She continued to look for ways to offer him encouragement and support as opposed to undermining his manhood or self-worth. Her humble yet strong faith and determination would pay off.

I find that few wives truly understand the depth of their influence and impact on their husbands' minds and hearts.

However, the truth is that a loving and supportive wife who understands God's plan for marriage is a tool in God's hands to help mold and shape her husband into the man God created him to be.

Soon Melissa was encouraged to see the same principle that she had watched throughout her life in the garden take place in her husband's heart. The law of sowing and reaping. She had continued to sow love and respect in Cain's heart and life in many ways. Honestly, there were numerous days that she simply made the choice to do so rather than following her feelings, which would have said the contrary. Scripture gives examples of how one may sow a seed; another person will water it and then God will give an increase.

She surely did not see it coming, but their pastor in his new Sunday series on The Christian Family, watered the seed and soon, it was as though the Lord himself gave the increase. For the first time in a month, Cain asked Melissa if she would like to do something together on Saturday, his day off, instead of him playing golf with his buddies. Of course, she loved the idea and quickly accepted the invitation! They went for a relaxing ride through the country which Cain knew that she would thoroughly enjoy. They eventually stopped for a break in a quaint tourist town, went inside a local coffee shop to get a cup of coffee and a Danish, and then looked through a couple of the local stores.

As they were waiting for their coffee, they noticed a community bulletin board and they both strolled over to look at the advertisements and upcoming events in the area. At practically the same time, their eyes drew them to a catchy ad about a local garden and farm expo sponsored by a local business. With an excitement in her voice that Cain had not heard in some time, Melissa said, "Cain this is today, this is actually happening today!"

With coffee and Danish in hand, they decided to head straight to the garden and farm Expo. In the wisest and most selfless decision Cain had made in a long time, he encouraged Melissa to enjoy herself and to look around at all the various exhibits. He found himself enjoying the residential landscaping exhibits more than he had expected of himself. But most of all he enjoyed the look on his wife's face and the happiness in her voice. As he continued to glance over as she would interact with the employees and other customers, it began to dawn on him how selfish he had been. Never once had he thought about taking a day off to help Melissa turn their yard into a potential oasis for her with flowers and more beautiful shrubbery and yes, there was room that they could include a couple of raised beds for vegetables and herbs.

Melissa had countless ideas after looking at all the exhibits and her heart was full of hope to be able to enjoy once again being outside and watching things grow. However, she realized she was not allowing herself to get too excited as she was concerned that Cain would once again crush her dreams and hurt her feelings.

However, her fears and concerns were soon erased when Cain asked her to step outside for a moment. Though she would have never dreamed that it would have been at a garden and farm Expo, she received her answer to prayer. Cain sincerely apologized for the way that he had allowed himself to change. He told her he knew he was a very different man than the one that she had dated and married. He acknowledged how self-absorbed he had become and how that must have affected her. He promised that things were going to be different from that day forward. He said, "You know, I've been attending church, but I haven't really been listening to anything that's been said and I really haven't been trying to please the Lord or you. It's all been about me."

As they were near their car, Melissa began walking towards the vehicle to find some tissues to wipe the tears rolling down her cheeks. Once she was composed, he gave her a big hug and said, "Today we are starting all over. Let's go inside and buy the items you have selected that will fit into the car. The larger items we will have delivered at their earliest convenience".

Soon Melissa was enjoying watching everything that was planted in their yard grow and bloom. It was therapy for her and something she constantly looked forward to. She especially enjoyed the raised beds that were built and the vegetables she was able to grow and she enjoyed cooking for the two of them. However, her deepest joy was what the vegetable and flower gardens represented, their renewed love and understanding of how to develop deeper emotional intimacy with one another. They had never felt so close together in their lives, which allowed her to take her guard down and trust Cain's decisions as she once had. This couple is now poised to share their lives and dreams together.

The encouraging truth is, if this transformation happened in their hearts and lives, and it did, it could also happen for you and in your marriage.

Chapter 10: *The Gift of Each Other*

Created differently to bring fulfillment, not frustration.

"Then God said, "Let Us make man in Our image, according to Our likeness; let them have dominion over the fish of the sea, over the birds of the air, and over the cattle, over all the earth and over every creeping thing that creeps on the earth." So God created man in His own image; in the image of God He created him; male and female He created them. Then God blessed them, and God said to them, "Be fruitful and multiply; fill the earth and subdue it; have dominion over the fish of the sea, over the birds of the air, and over every living thing that moves on the earth." Genesis 1:26 – 28

Genesis 2:20 states that there was no helper "comparable" to Adam. Here the word "comparable" means one who is a counterpart or the matching mate of the other. Some translations use the words "suitable for Adam". While Scripture unapologetically states that there is a divine order for the home, which always provides the deepest levels of security and peace when understood and correctly followed, too many have mistakenly implied an inferior purpose for women.

Jesus called the Holy Spirit our <u>helper</u>, who would be sent to aid us in the service of our heavenly father (ref: John 14:16). This is the same term that is used for the wife being the husband's helper we saw in Genesis 2:20.

The fact that humankind was created "male and female" clearly shows God's image was imprinted on both a husband and wife equally and that His perpetual plan for the generations will include both genders. Acknowledging God's plan for your life and home can put you in a position where your hard work and efforts not only involve "working hard" and "trying more" to achieve a successful life and marriage but also invite His blessings and favor, which can greatly increase any of your natural efforts or agendas.

For any of us to try to redefine "masculinity" and "femininity" is both foolish and futile. The Creator had no need or desire to ask our opinion or permission to validate His purpose for men and women or husbands and wives.

Even so, both genders are a glorious portion of His creation. Without question, the Lord has deposited specific and innate characteristics of Himself in both men and women.

"He who finds a wife finds a good thing, and obtains favor from the Lord" Proverbs 18:22

Scriptures in both the Old Testament and New Testament support the truth that God has established marriage and He did it as a blessing for both the husband and wife. The Christian home was also established for the benefit of the children as they learn from both their father and mother, who prayerfully are serving the Lord themselves and setting a good example. Parents may not realize it, but they are responsible for training their children in the way of the Lord and how to live a Godly life in their generation.

Admittedly, I have had some husbands look at me over the years and shake their heads, saying something such as, "I know that verse about a man finding a wife and it being a good thing, but I'm just not so sure about that. I can't think of one thing my wife has said I have done right in 10 years, and I finally decided that she will never be satisfied with my income. I am in the same line of work I was in when we got married and I have received raises and promotions as well as working extra hours, but she continually complains and compares me to some of her friends' husbands."

Also, I'm certain that many women will hope that one of the first things she can do when she gets to Heaven is ask the Lord why her husband was so different from her. At that point, many of the wives will assert, "You know him, Lord, You created him. He only had one thing on his mind, and I did not put it there!"

Too often a couple's emotional intimacy is threatened by their lack of understanding of one another, as well as God's plan for their relationship. I always try to speak in general terms when discussing different traits of husbands and wives. I may imply that <u>most</u> men or <u>most</u> women will have particular traits, but I am never implying that <u>all</u> men or <u>all</u> women will have a particular trait or even that they should. For example, I have known men who love to shop much more than their wives do, or men who would have a greater propensity to run up a credit card debt than their wife would. I have also known ladies who enjoy working in the yard more than their husbands do, or perhaps enjoy a sweaty workout at a local fitness center while her husband prefers a couch and TV or sitting and researching at a computer. All of that is fine and good!

It doesn't matter who does the dishes or vacuums the floor any more than who chooses to get on the riding lawn mower or wash the car. Simply discuss these topics, know each other's preferences, and implement a plan that validates both of you and keeps the needed chores done.

Even so, it's important to recognize the reasons we need to understand each other and have conversations that help each other truly recognize what we are thinking and need in our relationship.

Years ago, Dr. Willard Harley wrote an interesting book entitled, <u>His Needs, Her Needs</u>. Over the years of talking with thousands of couples, he began to see certain patterns that he made note of. After 25,000 counseling sessions, Dr. Harley made a list of the top five needs that most men have and the top five needs that most women have based on his observations. His findings were very enlightening, and I believe warrant being repeated as we continue on our quest for intimacy. As you read his list and my comments, see if you or your spouse fits into any of these categories or even remotely close to what your thoughts are on your marriage.

If nothing else, it certainly shines more light on why so many countless marriages are struggling with oneness or emotional intimacy.

Women

1. Affection
2. Conversation
3. Honesty and openness
4. Financial support
5. Family commitment

Men

1. Sexual fulfillment
2. Recreational companionship
3. Attractive spouse
4. Domestic support
5. Admiration

Though I will make some personal observations about this list, reading this book for yourself could certainly be a great resource for continuing to build your marriage.

I acknowledge that there will be many couples who will look at this and say, *That's simply not us.* Some couples may even feel that their greater desires and needs are essentially the same as their husband and wife's. That's wonderful! Embrace it and be grateful for it. That should enable you to walk in deeper levels of emotional intimacy with one another as you share numerous common interests in life. However, the truth is that countless couples will find themselves looking at the list and saying, "*Yes. That's us.*"

The Top 5 Needs for Most Women

Affection: God created women as nurturers who need to experience true affection in their hearts and lives. I believe that few women would disagree with this statement. Most women care deeply for others and often find deep satisfaction in being able to show concern and support for others.

Of course, our wives need to sense our concern and support for them on a daily basis.

Dr. Harley states that to most women, affection symbolizes security, protection, comfort, and approval which are highly important qualities to them. When a husband shows his wife affection he sends the following messages:

1. I'll take care of you and protect you. You are important to me, and I don't want anything to happen to you.
2. I'm concerned about the problems you face, and I am with you.
3. You work hard in so many ways, and I'm so proud of you.

A hug can express any and all of the above emotions. Husbands must recognize the significance of affirming their wives, as most wives can never receive enough affirmations.

I have witnessed many situations over the years where wives were left feeling misunderstood and unloved, with tears rolling down their cheeks and crushed hearts. It's unfortunate that a husband's compassionate and patient hug could have eliminated the heartache. Simply put, there are times when our wives need our intentional physical affection that has nothing to do with sex.

Conversation: I have already shared several thoughts with you about conversation. However, it's important to note that most wives hold good communication in high regard. Dr. Harley's list serves as another reminder of its importance and the fact there is no substitute for quality conversation in our wives' view.

Trust: Trust is without question one of the greatest pillars in developing greater depths of emotional honesty and meaningful intimacy. Trust is a great benefit for a couple walking in honesty and openness with one another. All too frequently, I have spoken with couples where the husband or wife wants to guard many of their thoughts, activities, or information such as their passwords on their devices. Now, there are legitimate times when certain levels of security must be maintained within companies that would not allow spouses to open and share private or classified information. However, many spouses, particularly husbands, refuse to share passwords and information for fear of the repercussions of arguments and misunderstandings over things their spouse would discover. In this day and age, it is very easy to hide a portion of your heart and life even from those closest to you. In doing so, however, an individual falls into bondage as well as an untruthful, secretive lifestyle that will change their personality and the levels of intimacy shared with their spouse.

Husbands so often desire their spouses to be vulnerable and spontaneous in their reactions towards them. However, in many marriages, wives are living with their guard up and minds filled with suspicion due to their husbands' demand for unnecessary levels of privacy.

That said, I would caution anyone to refrain from being suspicious or accusing their spouse of any level of unfaithfulness or dishonesty without factual evidence. You may possibly be working through personal insecurities, past hurt, or disappointment that affects your judgment. However, there is tremendous freedom and liberty that comes while walking in the light of truth with one another in all aspects of your relationship. Sharing life with an open and honest disposition will have you walking in greater levels of oneness in no time.

We often quote the Scripture, *the Lord's mercies are fresh and new every day*. We all are very grateful that He does not hold our past against us and allows us to start each day with a clean slate. We should also strive to have that heart toward our spouse and not hold the past over them, especially when things have been worked through and forgiven. The Lord is in the heart and life-changing business, and I would encourage you to always expect the best and look for the best in your spouse. That is what true love does. If an unfortunate reality comes to light then it should be dealt with properly, but choose to continue to walk in freedom, love, and grace on a daily basis.

<u>Financial Support</u>: There are probably many who would think that financial support would be number one on the list for the ladies, but I see everything on that list tying into our wives' need for security. Whereas many husbands give themselves wholeheartedly to working hard to provide that security for their wives and families, it is important to understand that wives are also in need of spiritual and emotional security as well as financial security.

<u>Family commitment</u>: A husband's commitment to the family, which almost all wives treasure as their greatest possession, will go far in establishing deep emotional intimacy as a couple.

The Top 5 Needs for Most Men

<u>Sexual Fulfillment:</u> When I shared the list of the top five needs of men with couples, few wives were surprised by the number one need. Often wives have rolled their eyes, grinned, and commented, "I could have told you that was his number one desire." However, there are other topics on this list that numerous women have told me they were surprised about, such as "recreational companionship".

Recreational Companionship: The truth is most men enjoy a variety of activities such as golf, hunting, fishing, restoring classic cars, art, woodworking, and countless other endeavors. We can get very passionate about these hobbies and yes, sometimes we must be reminded that too much of our time or money is being invested in them.

Most wives don't realize the fact that as men, we often want to share our greatest interests and passions with the one that we love, our wives. A gentleman told me recently about a boat that he owns and how much his wife loves to go boating and fishing. I know many wives who enjoy fishing with their husbands while others would never desire this pastime. Some wives would never consider going hunting with their husbands while others would. Many women play golf, but that might not be your interest at all. I will give a word of encouragement to all married women. Find a way to connect with your husband and share his hobbies. If he plays golf and there are times he may just want to play with his buddies, that's understandable. But there is always a place where you could ride with him on the golf cart while he plays a round and you enjoy the beautiful course together. The whole point is being together, not your love for golf. You could ride with him in the boat and enjoy the sunshine while he fishes one day, or go shopping with him in an outdoor store as he looks for new sporting equipment. Allowing your husband or wife to share their passions with you is another way to develop emotional intimacy. Sharing your dreams with one another must never stop.

And yes, there are many places and hobbies that husbands can choose to enjoy with their wives that they may not normally choose themselves. Go together with a good attitude and make memories!

Attractive Spouse: I would like to make an observation about #3 on the men's list, desiring an attractive spouse. I believe this statement is true, however, I would love to make a comment that I trust will take the ongoing and enormous pressure off countless women to look a particular way or to maintain a specific weight. Of course, couples should encourage each other to eat healthier and exercise more, but not with selfish motives or by demanding that our spouse try to look like a fashion icon. What most men tell me is they simply want their wives to look good for who she is and feel good about who she is. Most men will gain some weight and lose muscle tone over the years, and women do the same. I believe we should be sensitive to that and continue to be our wife's or husband's biggest cheerleaders and inspirations. Most husbands I talk to understand their wife's desire to dress comfortably and to stress less about wearing makeup or their hair needing to look perfect almost all the time.

That being said, acknowledge the fact that your husband finds great joy and fulfillment in your efforts to look nice for him.

Domestic support: If a man's home is his castle and his wife is his queen, then it would be understandable that different levels of domestic support would be important to most husbands. This is a good conversation for a couple to have and make an effort to share the same game plan within the home.

Admiration: Lastly, the truth that a man needs to feel the admiration of his wife cannot be stated enough. Many husbands often felt great admiration for their accomplishments growing up in the classroom or extracurricular activities. At work, many men are admired for their dedication to the company and/or expertise. To come home to a wife who is critical and unappreciative is more destructive than she can imagine. Her attitude and comments will continue to hurt and wound her husband and over time, he will begin withdrawing more into himself, sharing fewer of the conversations that she needs and building higher walls of protection from her criticism. Emotional intimacy will be destroyed.

The wife who learns to speak loving and encouraging words that build up and help develop her husband's self-worth will reap tremendous benefits from it in many ways. A husband is far more likely to stand up for, defend, and fight for his wife when he feels admired and respected.

The couple who wants to enjoy the endless benefits of walking in unity and oneness will understand that their marriage and relationship is not a sprint but it is more like a marathon. Every day, often in the busyness of life, we make decisions that affect our ongoing relationship. Those decisions can have positive qualities that strengthen and further develop the important components of our relationship. If poor decisions are made, they will certainly have a destructive and negative impact on the future of the marriage.

Chapter 11: *Embracing Your Future*

I am committed, let's figure life out together.

What do you want your future relationship to look like? Dream your wildest dreams and imagine the deepest levels of love and contentment in that relationship. Think about the love and happiness it would offer and the unexplainable depths of peace and contentment that it would provide. I can confidently tell you that in our limited understanding of what true love offers and what true love is, God, in His master plan and great grace, has all that you can imagine and more available for you and your spouse. The key is, are you willing to learn His plan and then walk it out?

"For I know the thoughts that I think toward you, says the Lord, thoughts of peace and not of evil, to give you a future and a hope." Jeremiah 29:11

Throughout Scripture, your all-powerful Creator boldly states that He loves you just the way that you are and you are to love your spouse just the way that they are as well. However, He has a master plan that He desires to unfold before your eyes day by day, as you learn His word and apply it to your actions and attitude. When you allow Him to truly change your heart you will look at everything in life through a new set of eyes. Hopelessness will be exchanged with hope, fear will be replaced with faith, and bitterness will be replaced with unconditional love.

In the same way that He strengthens us and continues to change our character to be more like Him as we walk in faith, our marriage is also a continual work in progress. It should always be valued as our most important priority in life, second only to our relationship with Christ Himself. Of course, pursuits such as parenting and teaching your children to walk in the faith, helping develop their unique character traits as well as using your creative and insightful skills in your career, all have great significance. These and other endeavors can all be a very important part of your life, but I do believe that Scripture makes it clear that a godly marriage for those who have made the covenant to one another should be at the pinnacle of your priority list, second only to your relationship with Christ.

Sometimes we simply don't know His plan, and we must trust Him to guide us and strengthen us to make the correct decisions as we share our lives and dreams with each other.

Larry and Deb reconnected at their 20th class reunion. After graduating high school, Larry enlisted in the military, where he served for eight years, and during that time, he met his first wife. Numerous deployments and the necessity of the couple having to repeatedly move due to their assignments took a major toll on their relationship. Unfortunately, Larry returned from an assignment a couple of days earlier than his wife had expected and he discovered that she had allowed herself to become involved with another man. She told Larry she no longer loved him and wanted a divorce. Shock, disappointment, and anger were just a few of the emotions he dealt with as he processed all of this information and prepared to move out and try to move on. After the divorce, he found a job where he could use his skill set and focus on building his career.

The next season of his life was challenging, but he had been trained to survive and overcome and he was determined to make it as he started life again as a single man.

Larry could be the life of the party and was certainly a fun-loving guy. His friends and coworkers always enjoyed being with him and many of them wished they had his energy as he was always on the go. He was willing to put in overtime at work when needed but in his free time, he could be anywhere from the fitness center, the firing range, or with friends watching a good movie. He loved to go see action movies that featured some of his favorite actors. Larry occasionally would date different ladies, but he never developed a close relationship with any of them. What those around him had failed to see was that he had put a barrier up around his heart and his life to protect him from getting hurt again. The anger and betrayal he felt from his wife leaving him, coupled with issues he had dealt with on his deployments, had created a dark place within his heart that he hid very well but that influenced him far more than anyone knew.

Larry did not even realize how this barrier had prevented him from getting close to those he had dated. Unconsciously, he was distancing himself from them while at the same time trying to develop a relationship with them. Unfortunately, this is more common than you may think. Maybe you have even done this as well.

Deb, on the other hand, had never married. As they became reacquainted at the reunion, Larry was thinking about how surprised he was that this attractive and popular girl from high school had never been married. As her story unfolded, he learned that she had attended college and obtained her degree with her sights on a successful career in finance. Deb quickly began to apply the knowledge that she had learned about living on a budget, saving for emergencies, and long-term investments. It all made sense to her, and she could not understand why anyone would not choose to follow that same path.

While Deb's educational and career path was headed in the right direction, her love life was not as successful. She fell in love with a young man with great potential but a limited desire to use it as he should. She often felt like she had fallen in love with a younger teenage boy who lived in a man's body. She frequently wondered if he would ever grow up and become responsible for his actions. The spontaneous actions and funny stories that had originally made her fall in love with George and decide to move in with him later became a source of disappointment and anger.

George worked and would save some of his money but with a very different goal. He wanted the vast majority of his income to go to his passion for playing golf and he would often try to talk Deb into taking another vacation they could not afford. His attitude was, *Let's put the trip on the credit card and we will pay it off later.* George wanted to have fun today with little regard for saving for tomorrow. Deb allowed him to pressure her into that one time, but each month over the next 10 months that it took them to pay for that one-week vacation, her blood pressure would rise and the two of them would be in another heated argument. Years passed by in a frustrating cycle that proved to be an unwise investment of her time and love. She was disappointed with George and his actions but was even more disappointed with herself. She and George both knew there was no future for the two of them and agreed to part ways.

Deb had grown up in a church and a loving Christian home. She had been blessed to watch her mom and dad interact over the years and knew what a loving and happy marriage should look like. And honestly, even though so many other couples were living together outside the covenant of marriage, she always knew deep in her heart that God's plan was for a couple to make a commitment to one another in marriage. God's way simply works best. And if she had ever forgotten that principle, she was certain that her well-meaning mother would remind her of it again. And again. And again. Deb sometimes thought, "Mom, I know that! You don't have to tell me again." Besides, her heart was continually reminding her of it anyway. As Deb was processing her future, she noticed the following information that was posted on social media by a friend. She was grateful she had seen the information this way so that she could process it on her own. It all made sense to her. The post went something like this:

"Generally speaking...

Married couples live longer

Married couples have a trusted companion to share life with and experience less loneliness

Married couples are healthier as they have someone to help monitor and motivate them

Married couples share their wealth and can build more financial stability

Children benefit from the influence of both their father and mother raising them together

Married couples have more satisfying sex lives as it is shared with one trusted partner."

That is the short version of the benefits of marriage, and they can be found on both Christian and secular social platforms. The actual benefits are endless.

With that being said, if you are in a season of singleness or are called to live a single lifestyle, I encourage you to find a good support group that can inspire you and be motivated by your caring contributions as well. Like-minded friends who are there to share life's great joys and challenges with are priceless. We all benefit from interaction within healthy relationships.

The unexpected reconnection that Larry and Deb shared at the reunion sparked something in both of their hearts that they had not expected. They had simply come to see their old classmates, many of them whom they had not seen for years. Sometimes, true love is right around the corner, even when you don't expect it. During the upcoming months, they built a great relationship based on what they already knew about each other and getting to know each other now in a different way as adults. Deb found herself so proud of Larry's military accomplishments and all his sacrifices for our country. He was disciplined and goal-oriented, and she couldn't imagine why his ex-wife had let such a special man slip away.

Larry was amazed at Deb's intelligence and work ethic. He saw her as a hard-working, brilliant woman with a bright future. Besides that, as a guy, he remembered her beautiful smile and the fact that all the guys in High School talked about her being drop-dead gorgeous, and in his opinion, she had not changed a bit.

As time passed and the couple got closer, they both began to feel they should get married. They had so much going for them and a lot in common. The list of things they appreciated and loved about one another continued to grow the more they got to know each other. However, there was one underlying issue that neither one of them had dealt with or rarely thought about as they had been back in a new season of feeling "young and in love". Even though there had been warning signs on two different occasions when there were sharp disagreements with each other, neither one of them wanted to rock the boat and threaten their relationship by talking about the obvious issue. The anger that both had suppressed for so long was the issue of potential problems and additional heartache.

Larry and Deb had a simple yet elegant wedding with their family and closest friends. They were so happy that they had finally found true love. The next six months seemed to be the best of their lives. They were both so grateful as neither one of them wanted to go through another major heartache and breakup as they had in the past. One evening over dinner, as they considered ways to move forward and continue having a successful marriage, the idea of finding a church came up. They discussed the idea and to Deb's surprise, Larry was not opposed to it. So, they visited a couple of churches and found one where they both felt welcomed, and that had a strong couples ministry. They knew that it would be beneficial to be around other couples with strong relationships and marriages. Deb began hearing people teach and preach on topics that she had almost forgotten. She soon realized how badly she had needed to hear these life-changing truths and how far she had drifted from them. She privately determined within her heart that she was going to rededicate her life to the Lord and do her best to serve him.

She had no idea what was also taking place in Larry's heart. Oh, he had prayed before, and he prayed quite often when he was on deployment years earlier. In times of danger, he had prayed for safety and protection. Two of the men in his unit also prayed, he knew one of the guys was a Christian, and the other was a Muslim. He didn't care who they were praying to or who answered them, he just hoped somebody would hear the prayers and get them home safely. Now, after several weeks of hearing the pastor's series of messages entitled "Christ the Savior", there was a transformation taking place inside his mind and heart. His heart was sensing that faith was required, but it was making sense to his mind also. He began to understand and agree with the pastor's statement when he said, "We all are broken and lost, and we all need a Savior."

Scripture says that Christ is the only Savior of the world, and something deep in his heart told him that was the truth. Larry prayed that simple "sinner's prayer" that stated he believed that he was lost and needed to be saved and that Christ had died for him and shed His blood for his sins. Sitting on his back porch looking out over the woods that evening, Larry asked Christ to come into his heart. He didn't know all that meant, but he was certain that the Lord would show him how to live, and he knew one thing for sure. He instantly received a peace in his heart that he had been looking for his entire life! Deb was overjoyed with his decision and what it would mean in their new life together.

It's important to keep this truth in mind, that those who are trying to live their best lives and honor one another as well as honor the Lord, sometimes still find themselves struggling with their personal imperfections or their spouses. The new spiritual direction Larry and Deb had both received was giving them hope that, as a new couple, they could begin to move forward with their plans and dreams. They both felt such contentment and happiness in their hearts they couldn't imagine any major setbacks or disagreements in the future. With all their heartaches and disappointments in their previous relationships, they were ready to live happily ever after.

All of us need to realize that countless issues and situations can come up in our lives and schedules that have a profound impact on our hearts and relationships. Learning to deal with conflict is one of the most important aspects of developing a successful marriage. Though Larry and Deb were at a wonderful new place in life, they were soon to be reminded that we must live every day with a willingness to support and respect one another as we work through our problems and circumstances.

A couple of months later the inevitable scenario surfaced that caused each of their pasts to collide. Deb watched one of the most difficult and challenging situations at work unfold she had ever witnessed. One of her company's clients had lost a huge portion of their expected retirement fund and it was largely due to a lack of research and oversight by one of her coworkers. None of it was her responsibility or fault, however, she wondered if the same thing could happen to her. And how horrible it must be to lose such a large sum of money that you were counting on being there for your future. She simply could not get it off her mind. Larry had even asked her over dinner the evening before if she was okay, and not wanting to bring her work problems home, she simply passed over the question and informed him that she was fine. But it soon became evident that she was deeply troubled.

Ironically, it was just the next day that Larry called her at work from a car dealership after his truck broke down and had to be towed. The dealership gave him a ride home, and he anxiously waited for several hours before he received the call to find out what repairs would be needed. As soon as the service manager began the conversation with, *I hate to tell you this,* his heart sank as he waited for the bad news. His truck needed an expensive engine repair, and he was advised to consider his options and to call them back in the morning. As he sat there thinking about the amount of money he had already spent on that aging truck and the number of miles it had accumulated, he decided that the best thing to do was to sell that truck for whatever he could get out of it and purchase a new one. He told Deb what he was thinking when he called her and asked her to discuss it with him that evening when she got home.

Larry eventually wished he had kept his thoughts to himself. Deb and her coworkers were called into a late afternoon meeting by upper management to discuss what had happened to the client's limited retirement fund. He was threatening the company with a lawsuit and her friend was being released by the company because of the way he had mismanaged the fund. On her 30-minute drive home, Deb continued to process the loss of the client's security, their disappointment, and how they must be feeling. Plus, her friend was now out of work and definitely would not be able to use the company as a future referral on job applications. Now, on top of it all, Larry was telling her that he had decided to buy an expensive new truck which would cut deeply into their savings and jeopardize their financial security.

   Completely unaware of anything that had been going on at her work, Larry greeted his wife with a smile and a hug but quickly realized how tense she was as she pulled back from his embrace. Her behavior caught him off guard and before he could ask her what was wrong, she verbally unloaded on him all the stress, fear, and anxiety she had been experiencing the last few days. It was as though her emotions went from 0 to 60 miles an hour in only seconds. He had never seen this side of Deb and it was something he hoped he would never see again. In the few minutes that she had uncontrollably vented both her thoughts and fears, he was beginning to feel an anger he had not felt in years and was wondering what he had gotten himself into. He was already dealing with the frustration of his truck being broken, how much he had spent on the truck in the past to piece it together, and now what it would take to make the necessary repairs. It wasn't as though he was interested in making a big truck payment either.

Before he realized it, he started screaming back at Deb while using angry and offensive words that had not been in his vocabulary for a long time.

By the time Deb had finished unloading on Larry, she sighed, "Just leave me alone and let me rest a while, I don't even feel like talking to you now." With his head still spinning in disbelief, he decided to go outside and mow the grass and give them both time to think things over.

Later that evening, cooler heads prevailed, and they both had some things to apologize for. When they sat down later he asked, "What got into you? What did I do or say that was so bad that you felt like you had to come in the door talking to me like that and being so inconsiderate? There was a time in my life Deb, when no one would have talked to me like that, or things would have gotten ugly real quick. Now I'm trying to live right, and we have been on the same page, but you made me wonder what I have gotten myself into or if we should have even gotten married. Maybe we rushed into marriage, and we shouldn't have."

With tears streaming down her face, Deb apologized for the way she had talked to him and then told him all that had been going on at work. "I was already thinking about the client losing their security and I guess I just started thinking about what if we would lose our savings also? I'm even surprised that it all affected me this way." As they began to talk about her reaction to the events and his reaction to her, a deeper truth unfolded. There was still a nagging fear deep in her heart and mind that Larry might start acting like George. "I'm just concerned that you're going to want to start wasting money and spending our savings unnecessarily. I didn't realize I was still having a difficult time trusting you for someone else's actions."

As they took a deep look inside their hearts instead of blaming each other, Larry had to admit that his loud and cutting remarks came out of a place deep in his heart that he did not even realize existed anymore. It was the thought that he was yet again being blindsided by another woman. He had vowed that it would never happen again, and in the moment, he had let Deb know he would not tolerate being talked to like that or deeply hurt again by another woman.

The conversation concluded with the two of them acknowledging that they both had work to do in dealing with their past hurts and disappointments. The disagreement had a positive outcome as both parties realized how much they loved each other. They agreed to seek the help of a marriage counselor at the church and work through their issues, knowing that it would make their relationship even stronger. They also agreed that the best thing to do concerning his truck, which already had extremely high mileage on it, was to sell it and purchase a good pre-owned truck instead of spending money on a new one.

Every time we have disagreements as a married couple, we should always be looking for a way to resolve the issues and improve the relationship in the long run. Choose your words carefully and your actions wisely, knowing that the depth of your relationship will depend on it. It's not unusual to need time to work through your emotions and thoughts, but always speak words of encouragement and respect during the conversation, even if the two of you have a different opinion. Having different opinions is fine and normal, but degrading and disrespecting one another is never acceptable.

The covenant of marriage is a serious and deeply spiritual commitment. Beyond that covenant are countless practical ways that we can encourage and develop wonderful memories with our spouse. The couple who honestly wants to enjoy life with their best friend must treat each other as their best friend.

It would be wise to think back to the exciting and enjoyable things the two of you did while you were dating and earlier in the marriage when there were fewer responsibilities, such as raising children. There were many things that the two of you loved doing together which is why you could see yourselves spending the rest of your lives with each other.

Think back to the day when your excitement about love was so special, it made you feel so happy and excited that you were sharing your life with the greatest person you'd ever known. Where did you go hiking, maybe skiing, or where did you enjoy a racing event for the first time? Did you laugh and sing at a concert or watch movies that made you laugh and cry? Was it a day in the mountains or perhaps the beach that you will never forget because you felt so loved and happy? Think back to the special restaurants where you shared wonderful meals and conversations that made you fall even deeper in love with each other.

Emotional intimacy is developed as you build your relationship on positive thoughts that unite your hearts about the past and leave plenty of room to dream about a special future together. The couple that enjoys both a deep and growing level of emotional intimacy considers their husband and wife as their best friend and confidant and refuses to imagine life without them. They plan their future around the interests and desires of their husband or wife and how they can continue to make them feel loved and appreciated moving forward. It is an extremely rewarding life when we understand the value of living selflessly. A selfless life does not mean that your interests and desires are not important as well. As you continue to show interest and attention to the details of your spouse's heart, they will become more appreciative and grateful for your expressions of love. This will most always create a greater desire within your spouse to love you in a more selfless manner as well.

A few may read this and say, "I've been doing this for some time, and it certainly hasn't changed my wife or husband's heart." If so, I would encourage you to plan a time for you both to discuss the matter with mutual respect for one another as the foundation of your discussion. Let your spouse know how much you want to honor them and show them love. There is also nothing wrong with saying that you need them to understand your heart. Have the conversation, and end it with a hug and a smile, knowing that you and your best friend have come a step closer to sharing more dreams together.

Chapter 12: *Defining Emotional Intimacy*

His thoughts and her thoughts on emotional intimacy.

"Honey, how would you define emotional intimacy?" That may not be a question most couples would ever ask each other, but it should be. It can become a window into the heart and soul of your spouse. I suspect that many of you will wish you had known your husband or wife's definition of emotional intimacy much sooner, the meaning that only they know and hold in their mind and hearts.

Understanding their thoughts can become a new launching pad for understanding that leads to new levels of oneness and unity. Here is your opportunity to share your true thoughts and feelings with your husband or wife.

I believe it is important for both of you to share as truthful and complete definitions as you can with one another. Also, it is of extreme importance that no belittling or hurtful comments are given when your spouse is being honest and vulnerable with you. Use this information to understand your spouse better. This simple exercise may even help you understand yourself better as you both think about and verbalize your definitions with one another.

My definition of emotional intimacy:

_____
_____
_____
_____
_____
_____
_____
_____
_____
_____

There have been times over the years while teaching seminars and classes that I have asked both husbands and wives to write down their definitions of emotional intimacy.

It was no surprise that the definitions and thoughts shared by the wives were usually quite different from those made by their husbands.

As we continue to look for more clarity in our hearts and marriages concerning the emotional intimacy we share, let's consider some of the thoughts that were important to others.

Let's start by looking at the way some wives define emotional intimacy. Husbands, you would do well to take the time to read these definitions shared by some of the wives. They may reflect thoughts that your wife is having as well and give you insight into how to draw closer to her.

<u>Wives' definitions for emotional intimacy</u>

- "Emotional intimacy to me is being able to talk about anything to my husband without feeling judged or scared of his reaction. It's a connection that sometimes is beyond words, it is my heart connecting to his."

- "Emotional intimacy is oneness between a husband/wife where emotions are accepted without necessarily understanding what they are thinking or feeling, yet having compassion toward him. Compassion leads to what is necessary for a spouse to feel/experience acceptance and move toward God's best. It's resolving emotional issues. This brings deep intimacy with God and your husband."

- "Emotional intimacy to me is our sharing the feeling of our hearts beating as one (togetherness). It is a love that makes you feel safe and secure. It is putting the thoughts and feelings of my husband before my own."

- "Emotional intimacy is the ability for two people to connect. This special connection should allow both the husband and wife to share their beliefs, feelings, hopes, dreams, and even fears in a loving, non-judgmental, and supporting environment."

- "To me, emotional intimacy means when my husband hurts, I hurt! Or, when he is on cloud nine, I am on cloud nine with him!"

- "Trust!! In all things! To be able to open up in all areas of our lives, we need to be able to trust the other person. Trust develops emotional intimacy."

- "Emotional intimacy to me is holding each other up when the other is down. Not minimizing each other's feelings. Being there for them at any moment even if there is something else you want or need to be doing. Sharing dreams and doing all you can to support those dreams develops deeper levels of intimacy."

- "Emotional intimacy, in my opinion, includes: comfort with a person to the extent that they know more about you than anyone else. The person that you go to when you have the best or worst news. Feeling so close that it leads to spiritual and physical intimacy."

Husbands, you must understand how important it is for our wives to feel a real and deep connection with us. You may be content with a relationship that allows you to focus on your career and/or hobbies and only occasionally have personal and meaningful conversations and activities together, but that will never satisfy most wives. Our wives are looking for a relationship that comes from a man's heart that is real and authentic. Deep in her heart, she is craving a relationship built on openness and trust. She desires and needs a husband who understands the value of truthfulness, compassion, and yes, sometimes even longer conversations that acknowledge her feelings, concerns, and fears. Life often seems unfair and cruel. Even if your wife is a powerful corporate executive or an adrenaline-seeking rock climber or on the front lines of world missions, I would suggest to you that all wives want, need, and deserve a safe and secure place to find rest and peace in their hearts and marriage through emotional intimacy with an understanding husband.

Ladies, the following definitions from husbands may give insight into how some men have learned to think about emotional intimacy and relationships with their wives and marriages.

Husbands' definitions for emotional intimacy

- "It is feeling close like good friends. We both are really happy when our schedule allows us to go places and hang out together or even stay home and work on a project or watch a movie. I think she feels closer to me emotionally when we spend time together and have long talks. To be honest, I feel closer together when we are on the same page sexually, and we both enjoy that time together."

- "It's hard for me to give the answer I want to give because of all the rejection I feel from my wife. I know it means feeling really close, like best friends who are committed to each other. I really love her, and I want her to see how hard I'm trying to make her feel loved and appreciated. I think my emotions feel more love when I can tell she is putting me before the children and her best friend. I know I can communicate better than I'm doing now."

- "Emotional intimacy is where we share with our wives where we are emotionally and why. Our openness should be coupled with a sympathetic/empathetic ear to hear her heart. From that, she feels understood and comforted, which shows her support and appreciation for where she is emotionally."

- "Emotional intimacy is knowing what your wife needs without needing to be told."

- "It is being able to feel comfortable and at peace with your wife. It's when we have the ability to communicate openly and honestly with her. Being able to be so open with her that you share every thought and experience. It is to let each other know how you feel on a daily basis."

- "Emotional intimacy is sharing the deepest part of who you are, what motivates you, what scares you, as well as what thrills you with your wife. Listening to those same things from your wife that she has shared before but without trying to fix them. It is learning to accept what she is sharing and to strive for open and honest communication."

- "Emotional intimacy to me is understanding the needs of your wife/husband and being willing to meet that need and also having the desire to do so."

- "It is when we are not ashamed to tell our wife how we feel or what we are thinking."

- "Emotional intimacy is when we actually listen to our partners and their needs and desires and are willing to work toward meeting those needs and desires each day. It is hurting when our wives hurt and feel what they feel."

- "It is when we can share emotions, and when one is feeling something, the other feels it also. Like, when my wife is excited, I choose to be excited with her even when I'm in a bad mood. We should do that so that we will not hurt each other. Sharing both joy and sadness with one another."

What a vast range of thoughts and definitions! However, these examples by the husbands and wives who shared their thoughts remind us that every couple is learning more about the importance and need for emotional intimacy in marriage.

Unfortunately, some individuals only see the importance of spiritual intimacy and sometimes can fall into the trap of fulfilling the old saying, "They are too heavenly-minded to be any earthly good."

Yet, others may argue that physical and sexual intimacy are the most important.

Which line of thought is correct? Let us continue in our quest for intimacy by looking for deeper insights into our physical and sexual relations as married couples.

Part III ~ The Gift of Physical and Sexual Intimacy

Chapter 13: *Free To Love*

My past will not define my future.

16 months of research, shopping, and discussions had gone into the planning of Eddie and Morgan's dream wedding. Yes, it costs thousands of dollars more than had been anticipated. The chosen wedding venue had drawn rave reviews from numerous wedding coordinators and glowing brides. The colorful cascading flowers were almost beyond description, and the bride was absolutely stunning in her designer gown. The songs had finally been sung, and the vows had been taken. Eddie and Morgan faced each other, smiling from ear to ear, and placed that sweet, anticipated kiss on one another's lips as everyone applauded and smiled.

After the ceremony, everyone enjoyed a delicious meal while the DJ played their favorite songs. The evening was filled with laughter, dancing, and memories being made with their family and closest friends. The photographer even captured a memorable photograph of Morgan as she watched the evening unfold with tears flowing from her eyes. It truly had been her dream wedding.

When the evening and festivities drew to a close, the couple were finally alone with the love of their lives, anticipating the beginning of their long-awaited romantic and fun-filled honeymoon.

Eddie and Morgan were young and in love. They could not imagine their storybook relationship and marriage being anything except loving and sexually fulfilling. Theirs was a match, they believed, that was made in heaven. Yes, truly, one for the ages. Over the years, this young couple did prove to have a very special and enduring relationship. They were very fortunate to have some great examples and mentors in their lives as they were growing up and were wise to listen to their advice, well, most of the time anyway.

Many authors and marriage relationship experts say there is about a two-year window of time that most newlyweds enjoy an especially loving and romantic season of marriage. Their focus is still on pleasing one another, and their playful attitudes promote an atmosphere that's perfect for hugging, cuddling, and sexual intimacy with one another. Most couples do not have a lot of extra money at this point in their lives, but they are still convinced that as long as the bills are paid and the car is still running, they can, well, just live on love.

Fortunately for this young couple they greatly benefited from the advice of their mentors. In addition, they had some slightly older friends who had been married for 10 years. Their friends convinced the newlyweds that they needed to attend a marriage enrichment class at their church on a regular basis. Years later, they were extremely grateful that they had participated in the marriage enrichment class, where they had learned countless life lessons concerning relationships. They had also developed friendships with other couples who had made their marriages a high priority in life and were willing to give the time and effort to learn how to have successful and fulfilling relationships. As friends, they all encouraged one another during challenging seasons of marriage. They even held each other accountable when difficult decisions had to be made to keep their marriage on track. One thing the new class had helped them to realize was that, in no uncertain terms, they had a lot to learn. As the years pass in marriage, almost all of us look back and realize how naïve we were when we were first married...

I would suggest to you that every couple has more to learn about developing true physical and sexual intimacy with one another. Any couple can have sexual intercourse, but many couples will never understand the depth of intimacy or its potential to unite two lives and hearts. Additional insights come from both life experiences and a willingness to continue to study and learn. We especially need to learn from the one who created all husbands and wives, the institution of marriage, and wrote the book on relationships. How surprising it is for so many individuals to learn that the Lord himself wrote the book on relationships and intimacy. God is love. He is not bashful on the topic of love and understands every thought and feeling you have ever experienced or ever will experience concerning love. Yes, even sexual intimacy.

It would serve us well to remember that the Hollywood movie industry nor social media had anything to do with the creation and development of physical and sexual relationships. They may have mastered the exploitation of them, but generally speaking, they certainly don't display an adequate or truthful representation of their created purposes.

Genesis, the book of beginnings, transports us back to the time of man and woman's creation. There, we begin to clearly see a picture of God's plan for husbands and wives, including their sexual relationships. Eve was literally a gift from the Lord to Adam, bringing him love and support, which enabled him to fulfill his destiny in numerous ways.

God's creative genius was fully at work in preparing beautiful and plentiful earth for man to live in and enjoy dominion over as he experienced loving fellowship with God himself and his wife. More than anything, what Adam and Eve enjoyed in the garden was their relationship with God and then with one another. How sad that the very thing that God wanted to enjoy with his children and wanted them to enjoy with one another was so deeply affected by the disobedience from the one portion of creation that was made in his image and likeness. Man and woman.

Relationships are at the very core and heart of who God is and what He desires.

Money, fame, or power will never fulfill the deepest core needs in a person's heart. That can only be done with a personal relationship with our Creator. The order of relationships beyond that is with a husband or wife, children, extended family, and others. All of them are created in His image as well, yes, even the individuals who offend you and live only for themselves. God will judge every heart. You're calling and responsibility is to pursue the proper level of intimacy or unity with others.

So, once again, let's look inward into our hearts and truthfully acknowledge how closely we are trying to walk in fellowship with our creator. I promise you that it will have *everything* to do with the companionship and intimacy you will experience with your husband or wife.

In this section of the book, I intend to lay a path of understanding into one of marriage's most unique and fulfilling areas. This area is physical yet, at times, non-sexual, as well as a sexual celebration of love and romance.

You were created as a sexual being. Nowhere in Scripture does the Lord apologize or blush at this declaration. To fully celebrate this gift of God to you, some topics may be beneficial to learn about and understand better. Also, there are most likely some thoughts, incorrect teachings, or assumptions that should be discarded from your mind.

It has been said that the mind is the most important sex organ.

What could be meant by that statement? Correctly understanding both the purpose and the purity of sexuality in a marital relationship allows two individuals as a couple not only to enjoy but to celebrate their physical union of "two becoming one."

There are numerous hindrances that some individuals face in seeing their sexuality and marriage as a celebration or pure. Let's address some of those issues first.

I have been doing premarital counseling for almost five decades. It is a tremendous joy and a huge responsibility to try to help prepare a couple for a wedding, especially for the marriage. Of course, we cover topics such as how to improve communication skills, conflict resolution, finances, etc. However, one very important and sometimes awkward topic for couples can be when the topic of sexuality is addressed. Some couples feel a need to discuss sexual issues from their past, and of course, we discuss their future expectations once they are married. This conversation allows the newlyweds better to understand their future husband or wife and themselves. There may be certain levels of anxiety or even fear to be addressed by an individual, and it certainly isn't uncommon to address the individual's expectations, some of which may be unrealistic.

I often discuss concerns and anxieties that the newlyweds may have. Those concerns may range from anything from their sexual performance and concerns of satisfying their spouse to unfortunate abusive confrontations in a past relationship. Because of the varied circumstances that couples have experienced in the past, I often address the issue of the baggage that many individuals bring into their marriage. Emotional, spiritual, or physical baggage can all have lasting effects on their sexual relationship with their spouse...

These weighty and sometimes debilitating thoughts and concerns can be complicated for some individuals to overcome. Some individuals bring spiritual baggage into the sexual portion of their marriage, possibly caused by well-meaning but legalistic parents or pastors who made them feel that practically everything they did except go to church was wrong and sinful. Unfortunately, when some children constantly hear that sex is dirty, sex is of the devil, etc., they grow up to become young adults who still believe this untrue statement.

The point is if you are married and unable to enjoy true sexual freedom with your husband or wife due to any issues connected to your past sexuality, they need to be addressed. I highly recommend that they be addressed now. Your loving heavenly father does not want you to live with guilt, shame, or any depression or anxiety because of your past. Not for one more day. I'm sure you remember the passage from Genesis 2:25, which says they *were both naked, the man and his wife, and they were not ashamed.*

Shame is a tool that the enemy uses to cause you to hide your true self from others, even your husband or wife. It can even cause us to want to hide our true identity from God himself. Your shame may come from internal thoughts due to things you have done or thought about doing, or shame could even be due to your perception of your physical appearance. Some individuals have shared with me how difficult it is for them to look in the mirror and accept themselves the way that they are. You must learn to accept that God has created you to be your unique and beautiful self. Some will be taller, while others are shorter than you. Some may weigh more than you, while others will weigh less. Our complexions and the color and thickness of our hair are different. And yes, some women will have larger breasts than other ladies, and some men are sexually endowed more than others. Be a healthy version of yourself, but don't exhaust yourself and waste your time and energy attempting to be someone else.

Let me mention it here. At your wedding ceremony, you repeated the phrases "I do" or "I will" throughout the vows. You said, "I will be your biggest cheerleader for the rest of our lives." "I will love you just how you are for the rest of our lives." "I will believe in you and support you for the rest of our lives." We can lovingly encourage one another to live a healthy lifestyle through exercise or proper eating without belittling and hurtful words discouraging our spouse and sowing the seed of low self-esteem. Quite the contrary, your words are to enlighten, encourage, and bring out the true beauty of your wife or husband.

Far too many individuals struggle to look even within their hearts because they are concerned that they will not like what they see or do not believe they can make the necessary changes. Feelings of shame or low self-esteem are all too common, even with individuals that almost everyone considers handsome or beautiful and have a life together.

Shame is a self-conscious emotion associated with feelings of worthlessness or humiliation. We have all felt shame in our lives due to various situations or decisions. Typically, while in a healthy spiritual and emotional frame of mind, we can deal with the causes of our shame through efforts such as prayer, a commitment to make better decisions in the future, and possibly forgiveness towards others or even self-forgiveness.

Thankfully, like conflicts in a relationship that are appropriately handled, healthy self-reflection can become a positive launching pad to a more mature and healthy lifestyle. Sometimes, unfortunately, shame takes a stronghold in someone's mind and heart and brings its crippling effects into their personal lives as well as their relationships.

I have watched shame or embarrassment from an event 20 or 30 years in someone's past rob them of the personal joy that Christ wants them to experience and their ability to be vulnerable and loving toward their spouse. Often, the circumstances being dealt with were sexual, but not always. It is not unusual for a husband or wife to know that something is just not right in how their spouse responds to them or refuses to respond to them, but they cannot figure out why. We are masters at concealing our deepest secrets. If you have successfully surrendered your past mistakes and sins to the Lord, continue to walk in your God-given spiritual victory. Enjoy His freedom! Enjoy your freedom!

Unfortunately, some of you have been victims of other people's selfish desires and actions. Those scars are not your fault and never have been. You are a beautiful individual whom the Lord has handcrafted to enjoy him and be a blessing to others. Your worth and value come from the Lord himself, and no one can take them away from you.

If you have been a victim of sexual abuse in the past, I pray that the healing grace and power of Christ flow over your spirit, mind, and body right now. Please acknowledge that you are whole and pure through his loving grace. Also, recognize that those horrendous actions and memories were not your fault. You have every right to live, love, and be a beautiful person without anyone thinking they have an invitation to take advantage of you selfishly. From today forward, enjoy the purity and joy of your sexuality. All things are new in him.

My heart was thrilled and broken when an individual once told me with tears rolling down their cheeks that I am over 60 years old and I see my value and worth now for the first time. How sad that the enemy stole this beautiful individual's worth and true identity for decades, but what a wonderful reminder that the Lord is present today to restore your soul and help you understand your worth and value. Please don't allow the wounds from your past to hinder the potential joy and fulfillment your future can hold.

Some time ago, I heard a young lady share her inspirational testimony. Her name is Christine Caine. Christine grew up in Australia. She shared the fact that there were already circumstances that could hinder her from seeing her value even as a young girl. For example, she lived in one of the poorest areas of her state or the entire country. It was challenging to make something of yourself and get ahead in that environment. When I recently began to think about Christine, I thought that I remembered how her young life was devastated by being raped at the age of 12. However, when I went back and recently listened to her sharing her life story, she was actually stating the fact that four different men raped her over 12 years. I sat in my office with a heavy and broken heart after hearing this. I prayed for her continued healing and that her story would bless and strengthen countless others. I wondered how any man could do such a thing. I tried to imagine the effects that it would have on a young lady, but of course, I couldn't imagine it.

However, by God's amazing grace, the Lord began to speak healing words of strength and peace into this young woman. She began to see and realize her worth and value in the Lord. She was created to be someone special and refused to be a victim. She thought about Simon, the leper that is mentioned in Scripture. That's what is known about this man: he was a leper. He was unclean and acknowledged that everywhere he went. However, this woman refused to be known as Christine the abused or Christine the raped. She began to see herself as redeemed, pure, a young woman with hope and a future, and that is precisely what she has embraced. You can do the same.

I will mention a few liberating truths that I pray you will embrace and allow to become a part of your healing journey if you are struggling with any issues from your past.

In his own words, Christ declared his fulfillment of one of Isaiah's prophecies from many years prior.

Luke 4:18 – 19 *"the spirit of the Lord is upon me, for he has anointed me to bring the good news to the poor. He has sent me to proclaim that captives will be released, that the blind will see, that the oppressed will be set free, that the time of the Lord's favor has come."*

On the cross where Christ shed his blood for the forgiveness of your sins and his body was broken for your healing, He declared with a mighty voice that was heard throughout the heavens saying, *It Is Finished*! Once and for all, Christ provided his rich, life-changing blessings to all of us who are poor in spirit and living with broken hearts. He boldly proclaimed that we are released from the judgment of our sins and the thoughts that held us captive in our hearts and minds. He brought sight to the physically blind, but this truth transcends beyond that to state that all of us who were blind to his truth or unable to see the hope that he had provided for us now can have perfect vision to both see and grasp the good news. No longer are we to be oppressed, depressed, and filled with anxiety, but rather set free and enjoying the liberty of the Lord and a new vulnerability in our hearts. The time for the Lord to pour out his favor upon you is now. Except it! Rejoice in it! He has done all of this for you!

As some of you read this, you can have a moment where you exchange your pain and shame for his loving grace. You will never see yourself again as you have in the past. However, I am realistic enough to know that it will also be a process for some. That's okay. You have obtained a solid, truthful biblical passage to stand on for the rest of your life. When shame tries to enter your mind and heart again and bring adverse effects to your life, you have a passage to quote that God will support you. We surrender our minds and hearts to his truth to be renewed and strengthened. Accepting and applying one truth at a time can change your life and the legacy you leave behind.

- So now there is no condemnation for those who belong to Christ Jesus Romans 8:1
- He is so rich in kindness and grace that he purchased our freedom with the blood of his Son and forgave our sins Ephesians 1:7
- Do not conform to the pattern of this world, but be transformed by renewing your mind. Romans 12:2
- So when the Son sets you free, you are genuinely free John 8:36

With a clean heart and renewed mind, move forward in faith, coupled with your new attitude and effort toward your personal and marital blessings of freedom and fulfillment.

Please consider obtaining professional Christian counseling, which can benefit your recovery journey. Another option would be to join a small group of other women or men committed to breaking free from their past. Always participate in a small group and ensure the complete privacy of matters shared with the group. Support and accountability can both be valuable assets in your healing journey.

In their book entitled <u>What to Do When You Don't Know What to Do, Sex and Intimacy</u>, Dr. Henry Cloud and Dr. John Townsend list these five practical tips for discarding your baggage.

1. Agree that you have a painful past.

Acknowledge that a painful thing involving issues that were not resolved has happened to you. If you don't work through them, they will prevent your healing. So, the first step is confessing to yourself and God that you have these issues.

2. Include others in your healing and grieving.

Seek the care and healing you need to resolve these issues from others. Pouring out your hurt to those who love you opens the door to comfort, encouragement, healing, and support.

3. Receive forgiveness.

Getting rid of baggage means being free of the guilt and shame of past failures and sins. God will forgive you for anything you have ever done, no matter how bad. The Bible promises, *for as high as the heavens are above the earth, so great is his love for those who fear him; as far as the east is from the west, so far has he removed our transgressions from us* Psalm

103:11 – 12. Your past failures and mistakes may also have alienated you from certain people. You must go to them, humbly confess you're wrong, and receive forgiveness. Once you know you are forgiven, accepted, and loved, you can re-enter life and begin moving on. (NG Obtaining forgiveness from an individual is both valid and biblical. However, there may be times when it is simply impossible to do that because of certain circumstances. In this case, merely present your humble petition to the Lord, and he will make everything right in your heart)

4. Forgive others.

Some of your baggage may be hurting you've received from others, perhaps your former spouse. You still carry pain, anger, and maybe hatred. You must forgive these people. Take your cue from God, who has forgiven you. If you don't forgive, resentment will eat at your heart. When you forgive another, you release that person from your right to exact punishment and retribution from them. You also release your baggage of pain and resentment in the process.

5. See yourself through new eyes.

Another kind of baggage is the distorted view of ourselves we learned in past relationships or situations. We tend to see ourselves through the eyes of others who are important to us. And depending on whether that view is positive or negative, we feel valued or devalued. A realistic self-view will be balanced, recognizing strengths, weaknesses, and growth areas. Find this view by seeing yourself through God's eyes, for he loves and values you unconditionally. Add to this the view you get from those who love you as God does. Let this *New You* replace the distorted picture that has caused you such grief. Holding onto the baggage of the past will hinder your resolution of relationship problems that can impair your sex life. Ask God to help you leave it behind.

Chapter 14: *Hindrances To Intimacy*

Making sexual wholeness your goal.

Beyond anyone's mistakes in the past or abusive issues, other concerns hinder sexual intimacy in marriages also. I will address a few of them.

First, let's address the image of sex in general that some individuals may have in their minds and hearts. We often struggle as parents to know when and how to have "the talk" with our children about sex. A more proper approach would be having ongoing "talks" that would be age-appropriate. Just recently, a concerned dad obtained some material from me that would be beneficial in describing sexuality from a pure and biblical position to his son. Some parents did not share anything with their children to prepare their young minds and hearts.

When a couple commits to marriage, their insight and background concerning sexuality may be extremely different. Some young people grew up in a home where love and affection were openly displayed as mom and dad would share hugs or kisses in front of the family. Others, however, grew up with absolutely no display of affection from their parents. Yet others grew up in a home where sex was talked about as dirty and disgusting. It was never to be discussed and was seen as something God had nothing to do with. It's incredible that some of these parents even had children with restricted attitudes.

This type of influence occasionally makes it extremely difficult and, at times, even impossible for a young bride on her honeymoon to consummate the marriage. Instead of a romantic honeymoon with a lifetime of wonderful memories, there are those couples who experience a honeymoon filled with frustration, rejection, and tears. Usually, it's the young bride who is unable to give herself to her husband as she had hoped to and that he had eagerly looked forward to. Some couples have struggled with this issue for weeks or months before they can successfully come together and enjoy some level of sexual intimacy. It was and will continue to be a process for them. Situations like this, of course, require patience and understanding for the young bride and groom to be able to heal from past teachings and influences that hinder true biblical sexual freedom.

Various physical or medical issues may also prevent a couple from enjoying their sexual intimacy. I will list just a few, but I trust it serves as a reminder that if there are any type of physical or psychological factors that hinder or prevent sexual intimacy in your marriage, you should contact your doctor or healthcare provider at your earliest convenience. There may be far more means and methods that can lead to your complete healing or vast improvement with the physical or psychological issues that confront you leading to a healthy sexual relationship.

I still sense despair when I think about the gentleman that I talked to on numerous occasions about obtaining medical help for his problems with ED. He said he was too embarrassed and ashamed to discuss it with his doctor. He wanted to handle it on his own and felt like he should be able to do that as a man. However, as a man, his responsibility was to dig deep, swallow his pride, and get the help that he needed. I personally believe that the lack of male influence in his life growing up, a medical issue, and growing stress concerning his lack of ability to perform all contributed to his inability to be the lover his wife wanted and needed. Years went by with him ignoring the issue. Unfortunately, throughout these years, his wife continued to feel more unloved and less attractive. Eventually, feeling rejected and unneeded, she left. It wasn't that they just did not have sex; it was the continual thoughts and voices in her head that took its toll. I'm not wanted. I'm not loved. I'm not attractive enough. I'm not good enough. There are countless lies that often permeate a wife or husband's mind when they live in constant sexual rejection. The sad thing is, there's almost always help available if it is desired and pursued.

According to Web MD, sexual dysfunction is a common problem among both men and women. It can be caused by physical problems, including fatigue or pain, as well as medical conditions, such as heart disease, diabetes, and hormone imbalances, or by psychological problems, like anxiety, depression, and the effects of past trauma. Side effects from many medications may also hinder one's ability to perform sexually.

For example, the high blood sugar levels associated with diabetes may damage blood vessels and nerves over a period of time. This can hinder blood flow to a person's sex organs. This may create problems in men with both erection and ejaculation. Women may have a loss of desire, vaginal dryness, painful intercourse, and orgasm troubles due to the condition.

Damage to blood vessels leading to sexual problems is also associated with heart disease. Additionally, some medications designed to help with high blood pressure may cause issues themselves. Lifestyle changes such as diet and fitness can often improve the symptoms for many individuals. Individuals who have suffered a heart attack or dealt with other heart issues may deal with elevated stress over how vigorous sex may affect their heart. Candid discussions with one's doctor and prayer can help with these concerns.

It's also noteworthy that your mind and body go hand-in-hand. One of the symptoms of depression can be a drop in someone's sex drive. Additionally, some antidepressants can hinder desire and lead to erection issues in men. For them, lowering the dose of the prescribed medication or switching meds may be helpful. Talking with a counselor, making lifestyle changes, and following your doctor's advice concerning treatment plans, including medications and prayer, are all helpful components of a healthier future.

When you or your spouse are affected by the "C" word, all priorities change. Unfortunately, many of our marriages and relationships have been affected by cancer in either the husband or the wife. When that word is mentioned, and the diagnosis is given, sexual intimacy may well become one of the furthest things from your mind.

In time, when a person does become ready to be intimate with their spouse again, unfortunately, the disease itself and some of its treatments may make normal sexual intimacy more challenging. Chemo may make you too tired or sick for sex as well as adversely affect testosterone or estrogen production and levels. This could move a wife toward perimenopause or menopause prematurely. There may be ongoing pain and discomfort. Hormone therapies may also affect your sex drive, in addition to some surgeries affecting your body image.

Low testosterone is an issue that affects many men and their sexual fulfillment. It is estimated that up to 40% of all men ages 45 and older are affected by declining testosterone levels. Type II diabetes, as well as liver or kidney disease, affects male testosterone levels. However, a problem could even occur in the way areas in the brain communicate with the testes to make testosterone. Low testosterone in younger males is not as often, but it is also a genuine issue for some men. Low T in younger males is typically due to an underlying health condition or an injury. Testosterone replacement treatment (TRT) is designed to replace the testosterone that a man's body is unable to produce and to keep up with the general demands of the body. It is the most common treatment for men in their 20s affected with low T.

Let me summarize these thoughts concerning medical or psychological issues or any hindering factors concerning your sexual wholeness. Never underestimate the power of prayer. Never underestimate the benefits of ongoing, truthful, and heartfelt communication about your needs, issues, or concerns. Stop hiding like Adam and Eve in the garden. Expose your true self to your husband or wife and let them into your heart and mind. There is no shame in what you feel or what you fear. You're married. **You do not have the option of acting selfishly and ignoring the heart and needs of your spouse.** That being said, I want to give one additional word of encouragement and hope to those who have simply "turned off" or "shut down" their interest and desire to be sexually intimate with their spouse.

Ongoing disagreements over the subject, leading to arguments, causing hurt feelings and rejection, often take a debilitating toll on too many husbands and wives. Concluding that it's not worth the risk of being hurt or rejected again, some husbands and wives simply quit asking for their spouse's sexual love or offering themselves to their spouse. At first, days or weeks go by, but then the hurt or offended spouse realizes it is now being counted by months, even years, with no sexual intimacy with their husband and wife. It's time to re-evaluate your own heart and the heart of your spouse, and both receive and offer unconditional forgiveness to one another. Our Lord of new beginnings can awaken feelings and desires buried deep within your hearts and minds and begin a new stirring of sexual desire within you both. You both honestly need this awakening of your passionate love far more than you realize.

Don't allow a hard heart or a difficult season of misunderstanding or even intentional rejection in the past to dictate you're present and future. Life is too short, and the truth is that love covers a multitude of sins. Even when you do not feel you have enough love within yourself, allow him to love through you and give you a new love for yourself that can produce a new vulnerability for you both.

We will always be working through different problems, issues and challenges together. That is the nature of life and marriage. The beautiful thing is you do not face it alone. As partners, as a team, and as lovers, move forward into improved spiritual, emotional, and physical intimacy to the very best of your ability.

Hopefully, you both are willing participants when it comes to making love and showing your spouse needed affection, but sometimes as a wife, your thought is that *that is all the man thinks about. I think he must have a problem concerning sex. I have to be honest. Sometimes it concerns me. I just don't get him.*

It is not uncommon for wives to make such a comment or possibly even get it in their mind that this is the total sum of their husband's desires and life's ambitions. Ambition to have more sex and great sex. Sometimes, this leads a wife to become frustrated and angry to the point that she does not begin to or refrains from expressing her sexual love to her husband, which will lead him to have a negative outlook on the marriage.

It's wise to remember that even hard-shelled men get hurt, which affects their attitudes and sexual responsiveness. When Dennis Rainey invited a group of 50 men to answer a number of intimate questions about romance in their marriages, he received responses such as the following:

- We've been married five years, and on average, we do not have sex. She won't even talk about sex with me. Yes, for most of our married life, I masturbate every chance I get when I'm home alone.
- We've been married 20+ years and have sex less than once per week. It's routine: same old, same old each time. How can I get my wife to have and enjoy sex more often?
- In the past 10 years, I have resigned myself to not engaging in sex with my wife as often as I would like to. We have sex every two or three weeks. To deny myself is a sacrifice I must make in our relationship. But the longer we go between times of intercourse, the more I am tempted to fantasize.

- When my wife turns me down, I feel rejected, hurt, and unattractive. I get so very angry.

Let me clarify a myth before I address the issue of why most husbands do, in fact, desire sex more often than their wives do. It is not always the husband who has the more frequent thoughts about sexual encounters and intimacy with their spouse. Without question, there are wives who desire sexual intimacy with their husbands on a more regular basis than he does. Possibly up to 30% of wives have more sexual desire than their husbands, according to some research. In some marriages, it is the wife who is trying to review the weekly schedule to make sure that the children are in bed earlier to leave plenty of time for lovemaking. She may well be the one who is thinking ahead and doing research about a location for their next romantic getaway. Once the plans have been made and the couple reaches their destination, she wants and desires his undivided attention. His time, comments, and touch make her feel complete like nothing else.

So that may not be the way it is in your marriage; however, it is in some. And regardless, if it is the husband or wife some of the dynamics are the same. One is wanting and needing more sexual satisfaction as it makes them feel loved and desired, while the other is having to make the decision to share themselves as a gift to please and satisfy their spouse, share themselves but with a frustrated and negative attitude, or completely reject their spouse.

So let's consider the husband who doesn't think about anything except sex, or at least in his wife's eyes. Is he normal, or as some wives have said to me in great frustration, is he simply perverted? Perverted? I have asked a number of ladies over the years. Do you feel at liberty to share with me more insight so that we can reach a solution for the two of you? As most of these wives would begin to share their stories as their husbands listened on I would honestly have to inform her that her husband was far more normal than she imagined. Not normally what the wife wanted to hear but it was the truth. Bear with me, ladies. I always made it a point to help husbands understand the issue from their wife's perspectives as well before they left the office.

At that time, we would have to discuss what perversion actually is compared to a healthy male sex drive. Most always, the wife is trying to describe her husband's healthy sex drive, which she feels is excessive, while he sees it as perfectly normal. Of course, there are some individuals who simply live for sex, which makes a normal sex life with their spouse extremely difficult because of their unrealistic expectations.

Once, a loving and supportive wife and her husband shared their story with me. The wife was willing to make love with her husband three times a week and even spice things up by making love in different rooms of the house as well as different positions. This would be an absolute dream for almost any man, but her husband had allowed himself to become "addicted to sex." Beyond the loving display of affection from his wife, he had still come to a place of masturbating once or even twice a day. This man represents a mind and heart that is thinking about and desiring one thing only. Temporary self-satisfaction. He lost the focus of true marriage, the joys of loving and honoring his wife and living by the principles of God's word. The sexual fantasies, the unchecked motives of his heart, and his overall selfish mentality cost him his personal peace in life as well as his marriage and family.

Sex is to be a loving expression of sharing oneself with another, but it is not God, and the Lord did not intend for it to be the main goal of anyone's life. Pursuing the Father's heart is to be our main goal, and as we do that, we will learn how to express our love to others as he expresses his love to us. Lovingly. Tenderly. Respectfully.

The Bible has plenty to say about biblical definitions of sexual sin and perversion. Still, again, most wives are dealing with a husband who simply has a greater sexual desire than she does and not sexual perversion…

Perversion comes from the Latin word pervertere. It denotes a turning around or a basis for suggesting that something is contrary to something else. Perversion, in a biblical sense, promotes thoughts or actions that are contrary to God's established word and truth.

Psalm 119:89 forever, oh Lord, your word is settled in heaven.

Matthew 24:35 Heaven and earth will pass away, but my words will not pass away.

Dozens of other verses further solidify the undeniable truth that God's word is the final authority on all things. Always! There are those in every generation who believe they are included in an enlightened minority that believes that God's word is flawed or archaic. Such are the thoughts of foolish men who will one day draw their last breath and give an account to the Lord for their arrogance and rejection of his truth.

Concerning sexuality, feel free to debate and argue the issue until you are exhausted. God, in his unlimited knowledge and wisdom, understands what love is and how it is intended to be used by those he has created in his image.

Throughout the Old Testament as well as the New Testament, God has warned against sexual relationships that are outside of the beauty of a covenant between a man and woman.

In our society, more and more men are engaging in relationships with other men, as are women with other women. At the same time more couples are wanting to cohabitate before marriage to either get to know each other better or to become more financially stable before they are married. The statistics always prove that the results of cohabitation do not bring the more positive results of marriage. Regardless of the topic or the generation in which we live, Scripture remains the same.

Romans Ch. 1: 26 – 28, because of this, God gave them over to the shameful lust. Even their women exchanged their natural sexual relationships for unnatural ones. In the same way, the men also abandoned natural relations with women and were inflamed with lust for one another. Men committed shameful acts with other men and received in themselves the due penalty for their era. Furthermore, just as they did not think it worthwhile to retain the knowledge of God, God gave them over to a depraved mind so that they do what ought not to be done.

One couple especially comes to my mind that knows the depth of this unbridled passion more than most. This wonderful couple met as each one was in a season of grieving and asking the Lord for true love as her ex-husband had left her for another man, and in a completely different place and scenario, his ex-wife left him for another woman. Undoubtedly, getting to know each other and building a trusting relationship looked different from that of many other couples. Both of their hearts and families had been abandoned and crushed by what Scripture calls unnatural passions. Understanding God's master plan for marriage led this man and woman to make a lasting commitment to one another for life, and the Lord has greatly blessed them since then.

Condemnation from the Lord concerning your journey with a same-sex partner. No, nor for me. However, it is contrary to his eternal plan, which calls you to realize that and repent from rejecting his plan and accept his created purpose for both males and females.

I personally know what it is to deeply care about and care for an individual dying of AIDS and all of its pain and complications. I need not describe the debilitating effects the disease had on this individual, but I supported them in every agonizing step of the journey. You would be wasting your breath to say that any of my comments are condemning or that I am homophobic in any way. Christ loves everyone and I do my best to do the same. But his word is yes and no. It doesn't change because of any of our feelings or experiences. I know that we can wholeheartedly care for someone and love someone and yet disagree with their beliefs. Scripture states that God shares his eternal truth so that we may understand his heart and mind and receive his best blessings and favor. He loves everyone enough to warn us when we do wrong as well as share corrective measures leading to his best blessings. God ordained marriage between a man and woman before the beginning of time, and his mind and heart will never change about that.

Scripture also sternly warns those with no regard for his word who have slipped to the depths of incest and even bestiality by doing the unimaginable. Fornication and adultery, which are the acts of having sex outside of the covenant of marriage, including those who would be single or married themselves, are addressed in numerous scriptures. These are the circumstances and issues that scripture addresses.

Hebrews 13:4 give honor to marriage, and remain faithful to one another in marriage. God will surely judge people who are immoral and those who commit adultery.

Scripture clarifies there are numerous ways that men (or women) can choose their own sexual preferences. Again, marriage is designed to reflect the holy love and covenant relationship between Christ and his church.

Additionally, there are far more men now (and women, for that matter) who, under the secrecy of social media, fall into the trap of visiting pornographic sites that are so readily available. Sometimes, something may honestly pop up in innocence, but the strong magnet of sexual desires often draws an individual back for one more look. One look can lead to another, which begins to release hormones that make this practice addictive and ongoing. Men normally hide in shame while looking at these sites, whereas others become so addicted and bold in their quest that they surf porn sites while their wives or children are in the same room, confident they can click the exit feature before they are caught. Gentlemen, if this is you, don't play with this fire any longer. You will get burned. Also, if you are a married man, you have a calling and responsibility to honor your wife and desire her beauty alone. The nature of any perversion is that it will take you further and further away from God's truth, purpose, and will.

With this being mentioned, I must tell and reassure every wife reading this. The vast majority of men tell me that they want to be good husbands. They want to be trustworthy husbands, and they want to be a husband that their wives love, trust, and believe in. Many men have told me that they are tempted and have to fight back thoughts about other women but that they are determined to do that in an effort to honor God and their wives.

Many married men live with a determination to look the other way and not allow the beauty or flattering words of an attractive woman to influence their thoughts and actions. But too many times, with looks of frustration and hopelessness, they will ask, but what am I supposed to do when my own wife constantly rejects my sexual request and tells me to leave her alone again and again?

I have often said that there is another vital aspect of agreeing to or disagreeing to be sexually intimate with one spouse. The "why" factor. The motive behind our decisions, attitudes, and words is always paramount concerning relationships.

Did the husband come across to his wife as somewhat preoccupied and a little short with her when she asked him to come to bed a little earlier than normal so that they could spend some time talking and cuddling? Did he refuse because he was upset with her for going over the budget on clothes again that month and he was trying to prove a point to her or because he unconsciously was stressing about finishing a proposal for a customer that needed to be turned in the next day she wasn't aware of?

Did the wife quickly stop her husband's flirtatious advancement as they were getting ready for bed because she was honestly fighting off a migraine headache he didn't know about or because she had become angry and frustrated at him for not helping around the house as much as she feels that he should? So, she decided that if he can't do what I think is a fair way for him to get some stress off of me. I'll show him what real stress can feel like!

Consider the different narratives even when a spouse is not sexually receptive on a given day.

Consider these conversations coming from two entirely different motives and attitudes.

Stop! I'm sick of hearing about it. If that's all you are going to talk about, go to another room!

Babe, besides getting up early this morning, I got involved in that deep cleaning in the kitchen today, and it has left me extremely tired and sore. I will do my best to get some rest and plan ahead for tomorrow night. Come here and hold me a minute and give me a kiss.

In neither one of those scenarios did the couple share themselves with each other sexually, but one went to bed feeling unloved, unappreciated, and rejected, while the other went to bed feeling loved, appreciated, and with a pleasant expectation. Honestly, in healthy marriages, even if the spouse in the second scenario who desired intimacy realizes their spouse was still more tired than normal or dealing with any level of pain or discomfort, they would be willing to wait yet another day but with hope and loving expectation. That deep level of contentment and trust concerning each other's motives and willingness strengthens a spouse in moments of temptation as well as enables them to live with an ongoing sense of love and commitment to one another.

Chapter 15: *We Are Created So Differently*

Understanding you helps me to love you.

Ladies, it may completely change your attitude toward your husband to understand that your husband was wired for sexuality even before he was born, and he had nothing to do with it. That is not to say that he is not responsible for restraint and maintaining a respectful heart and attitude toward his wife because he most certainly is.

Dr. Walt Larimore and his wife Barb authored the book His Brain, Her Brain. Dr. Lattimore states that the genetic, hormonal, and created differences in his brain and her brain occur long before birth and any chance of socialization. The resulting differences can be seen in the womb, throughout infancy and childhood, and into our adult lives. The unique characteristics of the male and female brain are maintained throughout life. Dr. Larimore notes that the structure of the brains are not only very different, but the brain chemicals are remarkably different as well. There are more than 70 different chemicals that have a major impact on the brain, affecting our emotions and responses. Two of the more interesting chemicals that affect the brain are hormones and neurohormones, which can impact his brain and her brain (and nervous system) in different ways.

A male's major sex hormone, testosterone, impacts his behavior and mood. Dr. Lattimore states that as a mood regulator, testosterone is a midget compared to a woman's major hormones-estrogen and progesterone. Nevertheless, testosterone is a hormone most associated with male aggressiveness, competitiveness, and assertiveness. A passive man, when given testosterone, will become more assertive and aggressive.

Testosterone, when given to a woman, will increase her aggression, but not as much as when given to a man because his brain is hardwired to be more sensitive to this hormone. Testosterone helps a man focus on a project, competition, mission, or venture. It keeps him from becoming distracted. Researchers at Georgia State University found that the "high performers" tested in each field (business leaders, politicians, sportsmen, and the like) had higher levels of testosterone.

I think the following information can help countless women better understand two normal aspects of their husband's behavior. Teresa Crenshaw, MD, an expert on sexual pharmacology, writes, the "loner profile" of testosterone is absolutely crucial to understanding what men are all about.... Testosterone motivates the male to strive for separateness in ways a woman does not.... It makes you want sex, but it also makes you want to be alone."

This in no way should give husbands a pass for being insensitive and demanding. However, it does answer a question that many women have asked me in counseling over the years, why is my husband so determined to be around me and maybe even be cute and flirtatious, but soon after we have had sex, he seems content to go out to his shop to work on a project or pull up some type of YouTube videos on rock climbing or fly fishing. Because of a lack of understanding and also because of the lack of better communication skills, this scenario has left too many wives feeling unappreciated or even used. Too often, the wife is saying to herself, well, his needs are met, and now he's gone again. This creates frustration and even anger in some wives. It may not even cross her mind that since he is experiencing fulfillment, he feels that she is as well.

Husbands must learn to be sensitive to the fact that their wives also have needs, and quite often, they may be different from his. It brings great joy to a wife to feel desired and to know she is appreciated and wanted by her husband.

Dr. Eric Vilain has conducted research on the genetics of human sexual development at UCLA. He stated," *We discovered that the male and female brains differed in many measurable ways, including anatomy and function. Sex chromosome genes contribute directly to the development of a sex difference in the brain between males and females. The male making Y chromosome directs the early gonadal tissue of the boy to become testes-- and it's the testes that are the primary factory for the production of testosterone that spurs the development of masculinity across the brain and body of the unborn boy."*

Many wives who understand the thoughts and activities of their small male children could gain some insight into their husband's behavior by understanding that he, too, was a little boy but now has grown up. We all have observed small boys wanting to pick with others, wrestle, throw things, climb objects, and so on. We also have observed countless young girls lovingly playing with their dolls or pets and almost instinctively playing mama to them. Often little girls will neatly line their dolls up on the bed and talk with them as they comb their hair. However, many times a little brother has taken a sister's doll only to pull its arm off or throw her up in the air to see if he could catch her.

Now, all of us as adults continue to be influenced by the genes and hormones that God has in his divine design used to create us, male and female, for his glory.

Dr. Lattimore states" *that the sex drive originates and sexual desires incubate in the brain. This is why it is sometimes said that the brain is the most important sex organ. A man's sex control center in the limbic system, especially the hypo, is much larger than a woman's and is highly sensitive to the hormone testosterone. Given that men have a larger hypothalamus than women and 15 to 20 times more circulating testosterone to stimulate their desire for sex, it's no wonder that the male sex drive is so powerful."*

This may surprise some of you wives, but many husbands actually wish their sex drive was not as intense as it is. Beyond the need and pressure they feel to be relieved during satisfying sex with their wives, many husbands deal with criticism and rejection from their wives on a regular basis. So often, faithful husbands have a deep desire to tell their wives they dearly love how desperately they feel they need their touch and love but refrain from saying anything to prevent an argument and additional rejection. Men, you must understand that if this is a reflection of your sexual relationship with your wife, you never have a right or pass to look for ways to have your needs met through pornography or a relationship with someone else. What options does that leave you? Options include prayer, counseling, reading informative books on marriage, and sincere, respectful conversation with your wife to help her understand your struggle. During this conversation, you should be open to your wife helping you to better understand not only her sexual needs as well but also how you can give her the emotional and domestic support in the home she needs, which can lead to her being more open to establishing a new understanding and mindset about your sexuality as a couple.

Alan and Barbara Pease stated," *There are few problems a man can have that great sex won't fix.*" Their comment may sound flippant or shallow to you. However, I would suggest to you there is a lot more truth in the statement than you may think. When most men leave their castles to begin a new day feeling loved and fulfilled, they are willing to spend the day slaying giants for their Queen. Hopefully, additional information shared in this chapter will, at least, somewhat clarify the statement's validity.

Fundamental biological differences are just the beginning of many, many ways his brain and her brain function differently when it comes to sex. Understanding these differences should help eliminate countless moments of frustration and arguments in the future.

- Men tend to be oriented physically; women tend to be oriented emotionally and relationally.
- Men can initiate sex anytime and anywhere; women initiate sex less frequently.
- Men are quick to respond sexually and difficult to distract during sex; women are slower to respond and easier to distract.
- Men need orgasm for sexual satisfaction; women do not.
- A man's orgasm is short, intense, physically oriented, and solitary; a woman's orgasm is slower, more intense, emotionally oriented, and (at least potentially) multiple.

Dr. Willard Harley observed that" *the typical wife doesn't understand her husband's deep need for sex any more than the typical husband understands his wife's deep need for affection.*"

I want to share one more fact from actual research reported by Dr. Larimore. A man's brain is so compartmentalized that when he starts having sex, he talks very little, if at all. This lack of talk during sex may cause a woman to think that her husband is not really interested in her - it's just sex. The fact is, it's both. During sex, a man predominantly uses his right brain. Functional brain scans during sex (yes, they actually research this) show that he is so intent on what he is doing that he is virtually deaf. No wonder he doesn't talk. That being said, men can and must learn to verbally express themselves to their wives with loving comments during intimacy. If you try to start a conversation with a man during sex, he'll have to switch from his right brain to the language center in his left brain and that's like slamming a race car into reverse. Women can successfully multitask sex and conversation, but most men cannot.

These are not boring statistics but in my opinion, rather enlightening truths that should help a couple to better understand one another and themselves. Understand and then embrace your differences.

Another important hormone that needs to be mentioned is oxytocin. This hormone, according to Dr. Larimore is often called the "cuddle" or "bonding" hormone because it's released when couples hug and cuddle. This hormone increases sensitivity to touch and the feelings of bonding, especially in women. The higher the oxytocin levels a person has, the less aggression and the more empathetic the person is. As you can guess, women tend to have much higher oxytocin levels than men. Oxytocin stimulates in a woman's brain what biologists call the "tend and befriend" behaviors as opposed to his brain's testosterone-driven "fight or flight" responses. When a woman feels highly connected to someone or something, this feeling, to a large extent, is enhanced by oxytocin. Oxytocin increases a woman's sexual receptivity and is partly responsible for her being able to have intense feelings of satisfaction during and after making love, even if she does not have an orgasm. When a mother looks into the eyes of her baby, her oxytocin levels soar much higher than a man's, and this oxytocin rush is extremely pleasurable to a woman. There is, however, one time when the male's level of oxytocin approaches equality with the females-- during and immediately following orgasm during sexual intercourse. It's his moment of bonding and feeling that "oxytocin goodness." The phenomenon of oxytocin bonding increases the longer a man is with his wife. So, for the male, monogamy actually can increase his bonding with and loyalty to his wife.

Let's continue to look at some of the differences and contributing factors husbands and wives deal with concerning their individual sexual fulfillment. Husbands often say she just does not understand me. I love her with all my heart and try so hard to please her, but she gets frustrated with me. Why did she not understand how important sex is to me? Does she just not care about me? Sometimes, the wife of the man who would ask those questions has her own questions to be answered. She may say, why is it so hard for a grown man who can give presentations at work or be the facilitator for our Sunday school class rarely be able to have an intelligent, meaningful adult conversation with me about the things that really matter to me? He acts so selfishly.

To prove his love for her, he climbed the highest mountain, swam the deepest ocean, and crossed the widest desert. But she left him he was never home.
    Alan and Barbara Pease

Let's look at some topics that personally affect our wives that most of us, as men, simply cannot relate to. We are hard-wired and created so differently that it makes some topics challenging for us to understand... Simply put, there are certain days in the month and seasons of life our wives simply need us to be more understanding and supportive than many men are.

While most men are somewhat more consistent concerning their hormonal changes, it is not so for our wives. For example, PMS is a normal and ongoing part of a woman's life until the season of life when her body begins to move into another important and life-altering season called menopause.

The medical staff at the Mayo Clinic states that premenstrual syndrome "PMS" has a wide variety of signs and symptoms. It will continue through a lady's reproductive years. It is estimated that as many as three of every four menstruating women have experienced some form of premenstrual syndrome. Symptoms tend to recur in a predictable pattern. However, the physical and emotional changes a woman experiences with premenstrual syndrome may vary from just slightly noticeable all the way to intense. Treatments and lifestyle adjustments are sometimes needed to reduce or manage the signs and symptoms of PMS.

Dr. Juli Slattery has served as a psychologist in residence at Focus on the Family. Dr. Slattery noted that since men cannot relate to PMS, they tend to invalidate it. She informs us that more than 200 different symptoms can be associated with PMS-one woman's experience can hardly be generalized to another's. She feels the first step in resolving monthly conflicts as a couple is to help husbands understand PMS and how it impacts them specifically. She noted that husbands may be insensitive to their wives' monthly mood swings because they see it as a catchall excuse. She reminds wives they are still responsible for the harsh words that cross their lips and, if necessary, to ask for forgiveness when that occurs. *Having PMS is not your fault, but it is your problem,* she states. *As such, take responsibility for* it. She said to wives that *when you get frustrated at your husband because he is not more sensitive, you are communicating that it is his problem. Instead, try a more humble approach. Honey, we both know that during a few days of the month, I am more emotional and short-tempered. I don't like being that way, would you please help me by......? At the least, give him a warning: it's about that time of the month, so I need just a little more space for the next few days.* He's likely to accept that much better than citing PMS in the middle of a heated discussion.

The list of potential signs and symptoms of PMS is long, but most women only experience a few of the problems.

Emotional and behavioral signs and symptoms include

Tension or anxiety

Depressed mood

Crying spells

Mood swings and irritability or anger

Appetite changes and food cravings

Trouble falling asleep, insomnia

Social withdrawal

Poor concentration

Change in libido

Physical signs and symptoms

Joint or muscle pain

Headache

Fatigue

Weight gain related to fluid retention

Abdominal bloating

Breast tenderness

Acne flare-ups

Constipation or diarrhea

For some, the physical pain and emotional stress are severe enough to affect their daily lives. Normally the signs and symptoms disappear within four days after the start of the menstrual period for most women. But a small number of women have disabling symptoms every month. It is believed that the hormonal changes within certain women trigger a menstrual period worsened by the symptoms of mood disorders. While some women tolerate their monthly cycle with less severity, others pursue advice and medications from their doctors to help relieve the symptoms, as many others research the benefits of herbal remedies.

Is it any wonder that countless wives have tried to explain to their husbands either through kind and informative discussions or angry outbursts from deep frustration with his need to back off from his demands or personal complaints about her attitude and try to understand all that is going on in both her mind and body? Men, most of your wives acknowledge the hormonal changes you experience. However, she is processing far more emotionally and physically during this time each month than most of us as husbands can understand or relate to. I'm sure that many Christian wives would love for their husbands to take the instruction in First Peter 3:7 to heart when it comes to the numerous effects PMS has on her body each month: *live with your wife in an understanding way.* If you want to know how your wife is affected each month by these changes, then ask her to share with you how the changes make her feel and what you can do to support her. While husbands are often wired to be sexually intimate any time through the month, most wives are not. Her sexual desire will be affected by her cycle, most likely from a range of not interested at all to having her sexual desire peak, creating greater anticipation for intimacy within her as well.

Much has been written on the effects of menopause on women as well as its effects on their love life and marriages. Perimenopause is the stage of a woman's reproductive life that normally begins several years before menopause. Menopause is the end of a woman's menstrual cycle and fertility when the ovaries no longer make estrogen or progesterone. Often, during this season of life, hot flashes and night sweats become a regular conversation in the home, with the wife trying to deal with these drastic hormonal changes while the husband tries to understand his wife. Mood swings, vaginal dryness and soreness, lower sex drive, and painful sex can accompany a wife's symptoms during menopause. It is a very challenging season for many couples, to say the least. A season that requires far more patience and understanding than normal.

As one couple explained to me, they had found themselves quite frustrated because of painful sex." *We actually discussed the issues more than we had ever talked about our sex life. In the past, there had been no problems; we just enjoyed being together."* Then the time came, he said; I was excited and ready for passionate sex, but the grimace of pain on her face let me know she was not enjoying it, *and we both ended up disappointed and not knowing how to solve the problem.* His wife commented that *"vaginal dryness was a new and unpleasant experience for her, but it, well, it's just the way it is.* She said they purchased a lubricant at a store, but it seemed to irritate her, and the problem persisted. She then stated that" *a friend going through the same situation had encouraged her to try virgin coconut oil, and that product* helped them resume their sex life. "Sometimes a simple change of mind in attitude or knowledge of a helpful product is all it takes for a couple to be able to regain their many benefits of sexual intimacy. If needed, find the product or professional guidance needed to help restore your moments of intimacy.

God bless our wives. When they start this journey into menopause, they only know the stories they have heard, the articles they have read, and possibly some insight from their doctor. I will not even attempt to describe the difference between their reality and what they had expected. Of course, there are a varied degree of effects on our wives but most conclude that it is an altering season of life for them personally and their marriage. However, I do know that as husbands who so often have tried to fix things in the past, we are now treading into new waters. Yes, turbulent waters at times. I have had husbands come to me for encouragement and advice with the complete range from brokenness and tears from repeated comments by their wives to extreme anger as their frustration would build as they tried to understand and support their wives but honestly did not know where to start.

I've got to share a personal story here. During that season of marriage, as my wife Suzy was going through menopause, she had horrible hot flashes and night sweats while I felt like I would literally freeze to death with her new thermostat setting at night, even though I added an extra blanket on my side.

She and I both eventually laughed about this scenario countless times, but it did not seem as funny at the moment. One Sunday afternoon, I was reading the newspaper, and I looked over the section with new book reviews. I literally saw a book critiqued on what men need to know about menopause. I looked up from my newspaper while also watching a ballgame on TV, smiled at her, and told her what I had just learned about.

I said *I think I would order a copy, being the concerned husband, pastor,* and counselor that I was. She looked at me and said, yes, I think you should order one! I don't remember her smiling when she said that, either. I did order the book and read it and found it to be very informative and enlightening to me as a man. Honestly, guys, we don't have a clue.

I made adjustments in my patience and understanding after that. I understood that it was no laughing matter and tried to only make lighthearted comments about this season of our journey when "she was in the mood to hear it". We honestly did learn a lot about life, each other, and ourselves during that season, and I felt we navigated it quite well, even though she did tell me one time about six months after I had initially read the book with a matter of fact look, that "I needed to go back and read it again!" Alright, dear, enough said, I'll go back and review the book, or maybe I missed something when I read it the first time.

There can be countless reasons for couples to have conflicts concerning their sexual intimacy. They can range from financial stress to a new and busy schedule of life with children whom they dearly love and yet drastically change their past levels of sexual intimacy. Children are a heritage from the Lord and an absolute gift in our lives. They are a product of our deepest expression of love for one another. When we look into the eyes of our child, it is forever life-changing. You see the power of God himself. You see a portion of yourself and of your spouse. You see hope and vulnerability in a true expression of love in its purest form. Our children are to always be treasured and valued. We so often recognize a new sense of responsibility in our lives and the reason for us to "grow up" and mature as quickly as possible so that we can lead and guide our "mini-me" through the challenges of life.

Of course, volumes have been written on every topic, from how to raise their children to how to enjoy our children. It may seem to you in the present season of life that you are always tied down in your schedule or experiencing excessive financial demands upon you to provide for the needs of your children. I'll tell you this season will pass, and it will pass more quickly than you realize. Embrace the joys and, yes, even the challenges of raising your children and keeping the very best possible attitude while you are doing it. You are a reflection of God's great grace to your child and the one who is called to set an example before them to learn how to honor the Lord, how to show love and respect to others, and how to become a husband and wife in the future. Make memories with your children continually. Don't get frustrated and angry if you do not have money available for the huge trips that social media seems to indicate everyone else can afford. Many couples are going deep into debt for these trips either to make themselves happy temporarily or to keep up with other couples who have a greater income. Make a plan to camp out in your own backyard or to take day trips, which allow you to make wonderful memories with your children and stay within budget.

While our thoughts are on growing families and children, let's address the issue that your sexual life may be changed for the season due to their arrival. After a baby arrives, the mother will need time to heal, and your doctor will advise against sexual intercourse. There may be sleepless nights and a realization that you're going to have to learn to share time, attention, and aspects of physical love with someone else. Even after a recommended time of restraint and you both are able to enjoy lovemaking again, there will be cries in the night and interruptions. These will go on for years, but it is a part of your "new normal". As opposed to resenting them, find ways to work together to embrace all aspects of this special season of life with his/her parents without ignoring your responsibilities and needs as husbands and wives. It will take more planning than it used to, and spontaneous moments of sexual expression may be more limited, but mom and dad must stay committed to one another and their sexual fulfillment. Too often, an unhealthy amount of a mom or dad's love and attention goes to the child while ignoring their spouse. This will develop resentment and rejection. Don't allow it to happen. Even your young children need the blessing of seeing their mama and daddy displaying appropriate affection to one another in their formative years. This develops a sense of security and the children that is priceless.

Also, there are those young mamas who find themselves dealing with issues such as postpartum depression. This often is difficult for their husbands to understand, who have such a tendency to ignore problems, acknowledge there is a problem but see no great need to deal with it, or simply cannot relate to and understand what their wives are going through. Compassion, empathy and patience are often needed as a husband supports his wife in a loving way to work through such seasons. Commit yourself to learning all you can about any medical or emotional issue that either one of you is confronted with so that you may offer full support.

There can be many sources of conflict and relationships, but it is extremely important that we find a way to communicate about them.

Dennis and Barbara Rainey surveyed more than 1,000 couples and were stunned to learn that more than 50% never discuss their romantic conflict in their relationships. Are you such a couple? In their book Rekindling the Romance, they pinpoint the six primary causes of romantic conflict.

    1.   *Wrong timing.* He initiates, but she's too exhausted. She takes the lead, but he's got a deadline to meet at work. Maybe both plan a romantic evening and then something unexpected comes up. Allergies, a crisis with a child or family member, or a phone call can put a chill on the evening.

    2.   *Different needs.* Frequency, variety, and creativity in lovemaking are constant sources of conflict. One wants more sex; the other desires less. One is content with vanilla; the other wants 31 flavors… all in one night.

    3.   *Different expectations.* When they finally get alone, she has a relationship on her mind. She wants to cuddle, talk, and share dreams for an hour, but it's been some time since they have been together sexually, and he wants to go for the goal. Or, when both are anticipating sex, perhaps he wants a five-course feast, and she wants a quick snack.

    4.   *Selfishness.* She needs to warm up, but he's already fired up. Or he's given all day to meet her relational needs, yet she selfishly withholds physical intimacy. In some cases, it boils down to a simple

unwillingness to be responsive to meet the unique romantic needs of a spouse.

5. *Fear and insecurity.* Many couples don't trust each other with such intimate longings. Maybe they have been abused emotionally or sexually, they have been hurt in a previous relationship, or they're afraid the spouse won't give respect when honest feelings are shared.

6. *Wrong attitude about sex, passion, and romance.* Some may have a twisted view of romance because of past abuse; they may think God doesn't want a couple to enjoy sex. Others may have developed a warped picture of intimacy from their obsession with porn or romance novels. Some women wrongfully use sex as a "reward" for performance when he, for example, does something on their honey-do list rather than as an expression of love and oneness.

Chapter 16: *Becoming The Lover, You Want And Need*

I'm surprised ! the Bible is the ultimate guide to passionate love and romance.

Let's continue to look at the wonderful plan of sexual intimacy designed by the Lord himself.

Marla Taviano, in her book entitled, <u>Is That All He Thinks About</u>? <u>How to Enjoy Great Sex with Your Husband</u> commented that sex is not equal to *men and women. It is not fair to judge our husbands according to our framework. They weren't built the same. His desire for sex is no more wrong or out of proportion than my desire for emotional connection and affection. We want our husbands to share their emotions with us, but then we often dictate the method. We insist they verbalize what they feel rather than express it physically through sex*. For a guy, *sex is emotional. It meets emotional needs deep within his soul.* She states that "*it's very important to your husband that he feels like a man. His masculinity is wrapped up in a handful of basic things, including his ability to provide for his family and his sexual prowess. Sex, to your husband, isn't all about him.* (Though some wives think it is) *It's about you.*"

How you respond to him is a huge part of his identity. Ladies, these statements are not coming from a man who thinks like your husband but rather from a

Christian wife who purposed in her heart to learn how to both love and understand her husband and encourage him as both a man and a Christian man. Her desire was to learn how to make him feel loved and focus on supporting his family and growing in the Lord. Another alternative would be for him to feel rejected and spend his time and energy simply praying to get along with his wife and avoid temptation. I also find wisdom in her statement when she acknowledges," *your husband doesn't expect you to be superwoman, just his woman."*

Lorillee Craker advises that wives understand that random desires from their husbands may not always fit conveniently into their schedules. She says *that when we gripe and complain about our husbands perpetually wanting sex, we are ignoring an important fact: God made them that way.* As the prophet Isaiah writes, *who am I* (clay) *to argue with God* (the Potter) *about his creation?* God wants a husband to be physically drawn to you-- like a magnet consistently wanting to be close to you. The song of Solomon states*, "I belong to my lover, and his desire is for me."* Solomon's wife did not say those things while she was rolling her eyes in frustration. She was thrilled that her husband wanted her. Lori reminds wives that you should be thrilled too.

In the same way, husbands should be thrilled that their wives desire them as well. Many husbands have wasted too many years of their married lives, focusing mainly on themselves and their pleasure. It's time for men to learn and experience the deep joys and satisfaction of learning to speak their wife's love language and making her feel like the most loved woman in the world.

I don't think I have ever met a woman, unless she had completely blocked out her emotions by some trauma or events that she did not enjoy being complimented, admired, and desired. Husbands would do well to acknowledge the statement I heard long ago, *"It's what you learn after you know it all that really counts!"*

We feel as though we know our wife's quite well. We believe we understand them and what really makes them feel loved and appreciated. But do we? How many wives, after years of marriage to Prince Charming, would acknowledge his efforts, hard work, and kindness but would still unequivocally make the statement, "he only knows part of me and never shows any interest in knowing all that is in my mind and heart." Unfortunately, this often leaves a wife wondering if he just doesn't know how to communicate about the deeper issues and feelings of their hearts or if he simply does not care. A husband not understanding how to communicate at the levels his wife needs him to is sometimes acceptable to her, yet often disappointing and frustrating. At least in that scenario, she has the hope that the "big breakthrough" in sharing their hearts may come at any time. Feeling as though he doesn't care is unacceptable, and begins the process of her feeling disappointed, then feeling unimportant, possibly even feeling used, and eventually angry, which brings retaliatory remarks and actions.

The stalemate then begins and escalates into isolation for the couple in all areas of their relationship. For many men, this journey to deeper conversation is difficult because the actual issue is deeper vulnerability and honesty. Many men are more interested in the outcome than the reason for it. Any wife who does not want to be a good lover to her husband has some issues going on within her own heart and life that she needs to deal with. However, the husband who dreams of his wife being a great lover needs to apply his heart to treating her in such a way and loving her in such a manner that it becomes easy for her to both trust and desire her husband. All wives need a safe haven. They need both a home and relationship that offers them security where they may succeed or fail, cook the perfect dish for the evening meal or overcook it, and let their hair down in both a natural sense and also emotionally.

Gentlemen, your girl just wants to be herself, and she wants you to love her just the way she is. Yes, she may come with her messy hair, worn-out T-shirt she loves to lounge in, loud songs that she sings in the car when she's feeling happy, and a tendency to walk through the room and tear up at a single scene from a good Hallmark love story. Yet another wife may say, that's not me. His wife may say that her appearance is extremely important, and she has no intention of going outside without her makeup and hair being styled. She would love to enjoy a slow dance with her husband in the den the way they used to, yet she cannot remember the last time they did it. And I know there are other wives reading this that say, let me get out on a pretty day with my golf clubs, my water skis, or evening my hunting/fishing gear without telling me I need to be back at a certain time to fix your meal...

Husbands, what makes your wife the beautiful individual that she is and that you fell in love with? Embrace it all over again. Some husbands and wives as well will have the argument; my spouse has changed. They like things they did not like when we first got married and want to go places that don't interest me at all. I know some husbands and wives who have given up on the relationship because they refuse to accept the fact that their spouse now enjoys the outdoors more than they did when they got married. Who wants to go hiking when there are so many boutiques I still want to explore, or I have had a stressful day at work, and I just want to stay home and play video games and think about nothing? Just relax.

Someone may say that in their early years after marriage they rarely even visited a farm. Now, after watching all of these shows on TV on homesteading, my spouse wants to have a garden and raise chickens. I didn't see that one coming and don't care a thing about it myself. Or possibly a spouse sought a degree and has come to appreciate a new understanding of academics and learning. Simple changes such as one wanting to watch more movies than they used to or a different genre of movies, or not caring years ago about music but now wanting to attend concerts are all problematic issues for some husbands and wives.

TOO OFTEN WE RESIST CHANGE. CHANGE THAT MAY WELL ENRICH OUR LIFE AND RELATIONSHIP.

Remember that the Lord calls you to be one but he allows you to continue to be individuals. You don't always have to love the same things, appreciate the same things, or desire to travel to the same places. We are expected to, however, love our spouses in such a way that we will be willing to do new things with them as an expression of our love for them. You should enjoy seeing your husband or wife excited or happily anticipating a new opportunity to do something meaningful for them. The joy in their heart and the smile on their face should mean more to you than almost anything. Enough with the selfishness in our hearts and attitudes. Let's learn to release and support our spouse in their new interest and adventures with a loving heart of support and happiness for them. Crushing your spouse's dreams rarely allows for an atmosphere of intimacy and oneness to develop in your marriage.

Husbands should want to love and support their wives in a way that creates a desire in their hearts to be their sexual partners with anticipation and true love. I'm certain that there have been many times that wives have made love to their husbands, yes, wanting to fulfill him and trying to make him happy but also thinking, I hope he will say some loving and kind things to me while we are making love or after we finish. I need to hear them so badly and he is the only one I want to hear them from. My love tank is empty. Apologies after arguments and rendezvous' in bed during the time of making up with each other can both be very enjoyable and bring needed healing to both hearts. Making love is a true stress reliever that bonds two hearts and bodies as nothing else can. That is all by God's design to draw us back together, again and again, as we face the challenges of life together. What we all are looking for, whether we realize it or not, is thoughtful and loving attitudes from our spouse that lay the foundation for that next kiss or hug.

Johnny and Robin went back and forth like a tennis ball for the first eight years of their marriage, trying to determine who was right or wrong and what was right or wrong concerning sexual intimacy. They never came to a point of excessive anger or criticism, as too many other couples have done. They simply could not get on the same page in their minds and hearts. They wanted to. They just were not sure how to.

Often, it would simply be a random comment or insinuation. They would walk into a large department store as Robin wanted to look at the latest styles in workout apparel. But before they left the women's section, Johnny would have her by the hand, guiding her over to ladies' lingerie. Johnny would suggest the two of them go out for dinner and a movie after hearing the reviews on the newest action movie. His top priority was to see the movie, not to be with Robin, whether he would admit it or not.

Robin would become disappointed that he didn't want to take her to a concert she would have loved to see and hear. He knows that it is one of my favorite bands and that I'm constantly downloading their songs. Why he is so unthoughtful, two of her best friends went to the concerts with their husbands. Apparently, their husbands understood them or loved them more. When they finally were able to get a weekend away, Robin greatly anticipated a relaxing walk hand-in-hand by the popular River walk. Johnny was so excited for the two of them to get out of town and be alone with no pressure from work; he was happy to pick up a packaged snack at the convenience store when they stopped for gas and go straight to the room and have sex.

Johnny sometimes would become quite agitated with what he perceived to be inconsistencies or" confusing vibes," as he would call them. He got to a place where he simply did not feel like he knew how to read Robins' mind or understand if she was willing to be intimate or not. At times, he would ask her or give her that certain look, and the next thing they would be in each other's arms, quickly moving toward a time of passionate intimacy. Other times, when he felt that all of the conditions or factors were the same, she would shut him down. Caught off guard, sometimes he would retaliate with a sarcastic comment or simply become rude to her. There were times when Robin also desired to be intimate and would respond quickly to his advances or possibly even initiate sex herself. Sometimes, he wondered why it is that the rules seemed to be changing all the time. Robin was having a more frequent thought that, though there were numerous things she really loved about Johnny, at the end of the day, he just thought it was all about him.

So how does a couple become more consistent in their understanding of sexuality? Most couples acknowledge that men and women are created differently and may physically or emotionally respond differently on any given day. Given the fact that our schedules are constantly affected by children, issues at work, or a myriad of other possibilities, a couple must develop a proper basis to make their decisions. Don't build your future decisions about sexual intimacy based on your feelings or hurt from the past. Build them on a rock that provides a foundation that will provide stability for a lifelong love affair. Christ is that rock. His word is that foundation.

Johnny and Robin felt like many of their questions were answered when they attended a weekend marriage seminar. They had never been to a seminar like this in the past. They felt certain they would gain more insight into marriage but never imagined the weekend would change their hearts and their future as it did. Truthfully, they signed up for the marriage seminar trusting they would learn a little bit and hoping that their spouse would learn a lot. Hopefully, a whole lot.

They assumed the first session would be on a topic such as communication or maybe about finances and how to eliminate arguments on that hot topic. To their surprise, the first speaker of the morning encouraged everyone to open their Bibles and turn to I Corinthians

7. Johnny looked at Robin and quietly said, what! We are having a Bible study, and then he gave her a grin, pulled her close to him, and said, *I was really hoping they were going to teach something that would get you straightened out this morning.* She looked at him with a grin and said, *yes, I was hoping the same thing about you.* They squeezed each other's hands feeling grateful and actually feeling loved by the fact that they were willing to come and to learn.

First Corinthians chapter 7 literally lays out a biblical guideline to understand some important life- changing basic principles concerning our responsibility and attitudes towards our spouse in regard to sexual intimacy.

1 Corinthians 7:1-5

Now for the matters you wrote about: it is good for a man not to have sexual relations with a woman. But since sexual immorality is occurring, each man should have sexual relationships with his own wife and each woman with her own husband. The husband should fulfill his marital duty to his wife and, likewise, the wife to her husband. The wife does not have authority over her own body but yields it to her husband. In the same way, the husband does not have authority over his own body but yields it to his wife. Do not deprive each other except perhaps by mutual consent and for a time so that you may devote yourselves to prayer. Then come together again so that Satan will not tempt you because of your lack of self-control.

Even though there was a large crowd in the conference center, the speaker asked for people to volunteer their thoughts on what this passage meant. One person spoke up and said it appears that the Lord wants married people to be the ones who get to enjoy sex. Someone else spoke up and said it appears someone's husband or wife actually has some amount of authority or right to their husband and wife's body. Then they commented, I don't remember it sounding quite that way in our wedding vows. That brought a good laugh from the crowd. Well, what does it say?

This passage actually teaches married couples that they should have sexual relationships with one another on a regular basis and with their spouse's sexual and emotional needs in mind. Also, it does inform us that when we got married and "became one" with our spouse, we laid down certain rights. Before anyone gets upset because of their aggressive or demanding spouse, usually a husband, here is the heart of the passage. Nowhere does the Scripture say that anyone should be abused, controlled, or taken advantage of. True love does not make demands in the same way that Christ first loved us and gave us an invitation to love him. He never forced his love upon us and we should never force our love upon our spouse.

What the Scripture does teach is that within the confines of a loving marital relationship, both a husband and wife will benefit from a relationship where they willingly lay their rights down in order to put the needs of their wife or husband before their own. It informs all married couples that there are great benefits that come from ongoing sexual relationships with their spouse. This willingness to share yourself as a gift to your husband or wife on a regular basis develops oneness and intimacy in many areas of your heart and relationship. Another very important factor is that it eliminates the temptations of finding loving fulfillment from someone outside of the marriage.

Scripture actually teaches that sexual intimacy is so important that it should only be stopped when an individual's heart is directing them and leading them into a time of deep spiritual prayer, developing intimacy with God, or intercession for other's needs. Some translations actually read that a married couple should only refrain from sexual relationships when someone is called to a time of prayer and fasting.

The Scripture instructs a husband and wife who have taken a break from sexual relations due to a spiritual calling to spend concentrated time in the presence of the Lord to come back together soon after the time of prayer, or prayer and fasting, has ended so that the sexual needs of their spouse and themselves are being met. In other words, even when a husband or wife or both of them seek the Lord for deep spiritual issues and growth God knows there are still natural, hormonal changes taking place inside each of them that should not be overlooked or ignored. To do so sets oneself and one's spouse up for temptation as one's emotional love tank becomes empty and one's sexual needs are unmet.

Unfortunately, I have spoken with a number of couples, and one of them would come in sharing with me like a preacher on steroids. They quote the Scripture, they talk about the will and power of God, they talk about their determination to raise their children in a way that is pleasing to the Lord, and yet they don't see a need for making sexual intimacy within their marriage a priority. In my opinion, these individuals have missed the mark and have ignored scriptural instruction due to their pious attitude and self-righteousness. Sexual intimacy within a marriage is ordained by God himself. And because we will always exist as body, mind, and spirit in this life we cannot ignore any area of our true self.

I'm certain this will surprise some of you but may also leave some wife saying, when I think about my husband this does not surprise me at all. But I have known different men who have surrendered their hearts to the Lord and truly wanted to walk close to him and be used by him. They studied biblical fasting and would pull aside for prayer and Bible study as much as they could around their work schedule. If you have fasted before, you know that normally the first two or three days are the hardest as your body is still craving sugars, various nutrients, etc.

The first couple of days may even have someone feeling a little tired or dealing with a headache. For those who have fasted for days or weeks at a time in the pursuit of a deep walk in Christ, most everyone would acknowledge that after three or four days, it becomes easier because of your new mindset and your body becoming cleansed from many of the toxins and preservatives in the foods we normally eat. That being said, the person continues to miss the joys of eating but finds themselves enjoying a more intimate relationship with Christ as they are focused on him instead of their normal routines.

I have had more than one man tell me after a week or even two weeks of fasting all foods and only drinking water and juices that if he had a choice to eat a meal or make passionate love with his wife, he would choose passionate love with his wife. But I am confident that he would be asking for his favorite meal immediately after making love with his wife. But these comments should at least serve as some indicator of how much making love can mean to a man. The Lord understands this strong desire for enjoying a sexual connection between husbands and wives so he says, make it a priority in your marriage.

Proverbs 5 gives an informative insight and strong warning to those who allow themselves to become sexually active outside of the marriage. This passage of Scripture also gives clear instructions concerning the romantic instruction for a couple.

First, the chapter begins by saying, pay attention to my wisdom; listen carefully to my wise counsel. The Scripture states, for the lips of an immoral woman are as sweet as honey, and her mouth is smoother than oil. But in the end, she is as bitter as poison, as dangerous as a double-edged sword. Her feet go down to death; her steps lead straight to the grave. For she cares nothing about the path to life. She staggers down a crooked trail and doesn't realize it. What a picture

Scripture paints compared to what you may actually see with your eyes.

Someone may see an absolutely beautiful woman or a dashing, handsome man who catches their interest. They may be one of the most enjoyable people ever to talk to. A great conversationalist full of insight and compliments. Just the type of person that you would love to be around and possibly even spend an evening with. However, the flattering words of this individual will bring you death, and because they have no conviction to honor marriage and are only out to be fulfilled regardless of who they do it with, their feet go down to hell, and their soul will as well if they do not understand the plan of God and repent and begin to honor his word.

So, God, in his wisdom, shares insight on how to avoid these downfalls. This instruction begins in Proverbs 5:15 _drink water from your own well-share your love only with your wife. Why spill the water of your springs in the streets, having sex with just anyone? You should reserve it for yourselves. Never share it with strangers. Let your wife be a fountain of blessing for you. Rejoice in the wife of your youth. She is a loving deer, a graceful doe. Let her breasts satisfy you always. May you always be captivated by her love?_

Though this passage has some Old Testament verbiage. I think it is clear to understand. The Scripture says let your thirst for passion be fulfilled only by your wife and your husband. Why should you become sexually engaged and experience a climax or orgasm with just anyone at some location outside of your home with someone other than your spouse? Clearly, the passage says never to share it with strangers but to maintain an attitude of love and respect toward your spouse. See your wife as your beautiful lover. Enjoy her breast, as that is part of God's plan.

Of course, there is a time and place for everything. Many couples have children running throughout the house, neighbors or in-laws in and out the revolving door of your home plus some have neighbors living very close to their home with all of the blinds open during the day. The statement, let her breasts satisfy you, always must be taken in proper context. But with that being said, it clearly implies that a husband finds great fulfillment and satisfaction when he enjoys his wife's breast in some way. A wife understanding this can make her husband feel deeply loved and close to her, whether he is caressing or simply looking at her breast.

A husband whose wife understood this principle told me this story. She shocked him one afternoon in a very pleasant way that he said made him feel so loved and caused him to see his wife as one of the sexiest women ever. He stated he was mowing grass in his backyard, and as he was mowing away from the neighbor's tall fence and moving towards his house, he looked up and saw his wife standing in their bedroom window. They waved to each other and grinned, and he quickly turned the mower to make another lap. This time, as he approached the house, his wife was standing in the window and pulled her blouse up. He said he almost wrecked his mower and could not get the smile off of his face. Knowing she may have started something when he came back toward the house again, he gave her a look as to say, do you want me to stop and come inside. As they knew each other so well, her look said no way, you need to finish mowing. He felt like one of the most loved and desired men in town. How simple and yet how loving a Jester it was by his thoughtful wife.

Always be captivated by her love. The Scripture informs us that we should maintain an attitude of excitement and passionate expectation toward our spouse. Captivated literally means to be influenced or dominated by some special charm or irresistible appeal. To be captivated by someone literally means to be consumed, fascinated, or preoccupied with someone. Does that describe your attitude toward your wife or toward your husband?

If not, deal with the issues of your hard heart, your disappointments, and your differences of opinion. Focus on the great qualities within your spouse and the things that you love and appreciate about them, and become more focused on the desired qualities. As you become captivated once again with their love you will find yourself being loved and becoming the lover that you know deep in your heart you should be.

Some wives understand the value and countless benefits of allowing their husbands to look at them and enjoy their physical appearance. Most everyone is aware of the fact that men are more visual, whereas most women are more emotionally motivated. Some wives enjoy presenting themselves to their husbands in beautiful and sensual gowns. Other wives may feel uncomfortable dressing in certain gowns or even feel like it is a waste of money. One lady made the comment that she would be throwing her money away if she did buy a pretty gown because her husband would want her to take it off within the first few minutes anyway. Why go to the trouble or expense?

Actually, the time and money would be a far greater investment than many women would understand. A visual image that is burned into your husband's brain of you looking beautiful and sensual is priceless. Long after the time of lovemaking has ended, he will be replaying the thoughts of your beauty and sensuality over and over in his mind. This creates not only a deeper longing in his heart for you but also a desire in his heart to find ways to please you. Beyond that, with the image of you in his mind, there is no place for the image of another woman.

Men being hardwired to be visual is another reason that husbands are so often asking their wives to leave lights on during times of intimacy. Again, some wives understand this and quite possibly desire it themselves, but then again, who wants extremely bright lights on as though it were some Hollywood production? Indirect lighting is often a great compromise and many have found that putting a dimmer switch on their bedroom light has worked wonders in helping to set the mood.

So we clearly see not only the suggestions but also the mandate to become captivating lovers. But admittedly, there are some challenges that confront us. Outside of a medical issue, there are mainly a couple of things that will hinder men from being as sexually engaged with their wives as they should be or attentive to their needs. One would be absolute exhaustion from a demanding job or even working two jobs plus his responsibilities at home. The other thing that hinders numerous husbands from becoming the romantic husbands that a wife need is the fact that he feels turned off or rejected by his wife. Her constant complaints and criticisms, as well as being unpredictable concerning intimacy, cause many husbands to just shut down. For some couples, when this wife finally is in the mood and desires her husband, he may not be interested at all. This leaves a wife confused and angry. All of this erodes the romantic love within their hearts and places them on a path spiraling downward. Something has to change, and that change will begin in your own heart. So wives need to be honest about how their attitudes impact their husbands. Even husbands who seem to be more preoccupied with other things in life or callused have a tender place in their hearts that needs to feel wanted and desired. A concerned and caring wife will find the words and actions that make him feel loved.

It has been said that often times men just need a place to make love and that women need a reason. Let's look at some of those reasons that are true in the heart of most women.

Dr. Kevin Lehman, in his book entitled <u>Sheet Music</u>, shared the results of a women's magazine that asked the question, "What's the first thing to go *when you're busy, tired, and stressed?*" If you answered sex, you're not alone. In the survey, an estimated 24 million American women say they don't have time, are too exhausted, or just aren't in the mood for sex, and more than 1/3 of Red Book readers say that being too tired is their number one excuse for not having sex. So, we put it off for later. Later can easily become never. In case you haven't noticed, absence doesn't make the loins grow hotter; it just begets more abstinence. Sex, on the other hand, begets more sex. Studies show that lovemaking elevates the levels of brain chemicals associated with desire. So the best way to increase your yearning for sex is to have it. Interesting thoughts from these ladies.

Husbands becoming aware of the physical and mental responsibilities that their wife carries is instrumental in helping her feel loved and appreciated. Lovemaking begins long before the couple enters a bedroom. Books have even been written on ways to make love "with your clothes on". Such books are an effort to help men understand there are many ways to make love to your wife. Help the children with their homework, help with their baths, bedtime stories, and prayers. Help clean the kitchen or vacuum the floor. Take the garbage out without being asked... Repeatedly. Keep her car clean and filled with gas. There are countless ways a husband can find within the day-to-day schedule to eliminate pressure and fatigue from his wife. Yes, husbands, these are true acts of love and sacrifice that remind your wife that she is loved... Always... And unconditionally.

Many wives live with a feeling of anxiety and some level of fatigue. Situations that range from world events to events within one of their close friends' lives or their children deeply affect the hearts of caring and nurturing wives. Sometimes, as a husband, we may make flippant yet well-meant comments such as, I'm sorry they're going through that. We will pray about it. But then as a husband, we move on and hopefully will throw up a quick prayer about the situation and move on to our next activity. This same husband may not realize that his wife has already formed a deep emotional burden or concern for that individual or situation. It's just hard for her to shake. While some husbands have complained and pleaded with their wives just to "get over it "or to simply "let it go, "that is not so easy for our wives. Some wives have described to me that their brains or thought processes are almost like a computer screen where other windows continue to pop up time after time. Often, I have heard a wife say, I would love to quit thinking about a situation in someone's life that is close to me or something my husband said or did that I'm having trouble getting over, but I simply can't. These thoughts keep coming back.

A wise husband will learn how to both communicate and comfort his wife when she is feeling stressed or anxious without having the goal of fixing the problem. Our wives are wise enough that if they would like our opinions or thoughts concerning working through a problem, they will normally ask us for them. Many times a wife needs an understanding ear and heart. I believe that one of the biggest mistakes we make as husbands and the lost opportunities we have to make our wives feel loved is when we fail to hold them in a time of brokenness, heartache, or despair. There are times that a patient and understanding husband can simply stand and hold his wife or hold her in his arms in bed when she needs to talk or cry and simply be there as her best friend as well as a source of strength and unconditional love.

Husbands who rudely or sarcastically criticize their wives in their moments of despair for crying and being so emotional have not only missed the opportunity to present themselves as their true lover but have also revealed once again how shallow their understanding is of their wife's hearts and emotions. The wife who feels a husband's physical and emotional embrace when her emotions are moving her in a negative or debilitating manner will most likely be the wife who can truly celebrate love and romance with her husband when emotions are soaring high, creating a loving encounter.

Our wives will choose romance over sex or romance combined with sex most of the time. For most men, sex can be an end within itself. Sex and fulfillment are the end goal and desire. Our wife, however, wants to feel desired. I still believe that there is a little girl and Princess in the heart of every woman who wants to be both loved and rescued by a prince charming. In no way does this take away from the strength and empowerment of any woman. But I have observed that even a woman who has excelled in her career with an annual income that most women and men could even dream of with hundreds of people under her authority at work still would like to come home and have her husband take her by the hand and lead her in a slow dance in the den floor to her favorite song, tell her how beautiful she is and how glad he is that she's home at the end of a long day. Yes, she thinks, make me feel beautiful and loved just the way that I am.

Dr. Kevin Lehman, in his book *Sheet Music*, mentioned the survey which asked women to fill in the blank: **if my husband were more romantic, I would be more inclined to**....

The answers were:

1. Be excited to be with him
2. Keep myself looking attractive
3. Find out what he wants; try to help him fulfill his needs
4. Stay with him rather than find a new partner
5. Be in a good mood around him
6. Attend to his sexual needs.

Husbands should improve their relationships by finding out what expressions of romance are most meaningful to their wives.

It's also very meaningful to our wives that we take the lead when it comes to making plans, such as having a date night or a weekend getaway. At least occasionally. So often, as husbands, we just say, take care of the details while we are walking out the door. But it takes things to a different level for most wives when their husbands are interested enough in making them feel special, and they take the lead in contacting the babysitter and making the reservations themselves. This says to our wives, you matter, and we are taking an evening that I can make you feel like a queen and take you out and show you off to the world. The same thing is true when a couple can finally get a rare weekend away. It's exciting for a couple to go online and do research about new cities and the activities they offer or brochures sent by the tourism department of locations that give countless ideas of places to go and activities to enjoy. The anticipation grows for both the husband and wife, but when you both can establish a date to go, many wives say it's one of the most wonderful feelings in the world to have their husbands make the plans around fulfilling their dreams and whisking her away for a romantic weekend. Some romantic weekends may include multiple times of making love and hours in bed enjoying each other's company and watching movies. For others, a romantic weekend will look different, but the weekend should contain thoughts and desires of romance that both the husband and wife embrace and share.

In their book <u>Rekindling *the* Romance</u> by Dennis and Barbara Rainey, the question is asked: what does it take to become the romantic man of your wife's dreams? The following observations are made.

- A romantic man engages his wife in a loving and growing relationship without losing sight of physical intimacy is an important part of that relationship and marriage
- A romantic man commits to learning nonsexual ways to love his wife while nurturing in her the freedom to be sexually responsive
- A romantic man can kiss, hug, touch, and cuddle without a sexual agenda while helping his wife embrace the joy of sex at the same time
- A romantic man does not pressure his wife into having sex, nor does he retreat from the pursuit of sexual oneness
- A romantic man connects to his wife's world, supports, listens, and shares his heart with no sexual strings attached while being confidently aware that sexual intimacy is vital to the survival of his marriage. A romantic man will do all of these things even when his wife is sexually unresponsive, knowing that he is called to love his wife as Christ loved the church.

Talk about a challenging word of advice. I remember a professor I had when I was doing my graduate work. He knew the stress that we carried as pastors, husbands, and dads. He also had the insight that, as pastors and counselors, we were never really off. In all honesty, there is not a holiday represented on our calendar or a time of the year that I have not personally been in hospitals or healthcare facilities or had people calling me or even coming to my door desiring help. All of this can take a toll on a marriage and family.

His advice to us was that we would block out one weekend per quarter to get away with our wives. The deeper word of advice was that we could only talk about our children on the way to the destination. We were encouraged to focus completely on our relationships with one another continually until we pulled back into our driveway.

Challenging, yes. Wise advice, yes. As couples, we drift apart, and if there are children in the home, we find ourselves building most all of our plans, activities, and thoughts around the children. Much of that is normal and understandable. However, when a husband and wife drift apart we are not setting the proper example of a loving marriage to our children. Also, the day comes when the children are grown, and that happens much quicker than most people would expect. Husbands and wives often find themselves looking at one another, wondering what they have in common, and when they lost that loving feeling.

Husbands, let me encourage you to take the lead in understanding the value of your wife's overall well-being. Sure, you told her that she was beautiful sometime back, possibly even at your dinner for your anniversary. But she needs to hear it today as well and the day after that and not to hear it as a recording being played over and over again but as a loving reminder out of your heart that she is still number one.

Diets and fitness centers are more popular than ever before. Proper nutrition and exercise enable countless people to maintain good health as well as feel better about themselves, which often leads to a better outlook on life. But the reality is that most of us change over a period of time. We gain weight, we are not as toned as we once were, and we simply don't have the energy and stamina we once did. Many husbands gain weight even without the hormonal changes that their wives deal with. In addition, many wives become mothers of multiple children. Understanding husbands will not expect their wives to remain the same size as they were when they were younger or before their childbearing years.

It doesn't matter if a husband makes a critical remark to his wife about her size while kidding or with a straight face. Most women will never forget the remark, if they do it most likely will be in the distant future. Too often, after multiple jokes and critical remarks, the same husband will be asking his wife to undress in front of him when they're making love or to buy skimpy lingerie. This makes it more challenging for a wife to do as his comments have created an unflattering and unnecessary self-image. Husbands, rejoice with the wife of your youth. Celebrate her beauty. Celebrate her love for you. Celebrate her own unique sensuality and do away with the unnecessary requirements that you have established or remarks about her changing physical appearance.

Let's be honest, we all should encourage and support each other as husbands and wives to take care of ourselves and try to be our best versions of who we are. That can be done without critical, degrading comments. It should always be done with edifying and uplifting words of encouragement and sincere praise for one another.

What does it mean to your wife to be romanced? Husbands would do well to understand the definitions their wives would give.

- Unexpected cards and sweet notes
- a walk around the shore of a lake or a hiking trail nearby
- dressing up and going to one of her favorite restaurants
- coffee and dessert with thoughtful conversation in a local coffee shop
- a gift card to a local boutique she's been wanting to shop at
- a spa trip that you arranged for her yourself
- a foot or shoulder massage that you would give her yourself
- putting money back and arranging for a cleaning service to come in and do a deep cleaning of the house
- having her car detailed with a good wax job and interior cleaning
- playing some of your favorite love songs and dancing through the house

And yes, most of our wives occasionally enjoy dressing up and going to a nice restaurant for a wonderful meal and kind and romantic conversation.

Flowers and chocolates and many other simple expressions of love may also feel her love tank.

Husbands, you get the idea. You know your sweet girl better than anyone. Make your list and start checking off the ways that you can show her how much you love and respect her on an ongoing basis, and, yes, pamper her every chance you get. She is a one-of-a-kind beauty, and the more you treat her that way, the more deeply she will feel loved and open her heart to loving you.

Remember that true lovemaking is an act of giving, not receiving. Always try to be mindful of your motives, not only your actions. With this in mind I want to emphasize the importance for husbands to understand that lovemaking can look quite different to your wives. Since men can so often desire and enjoy passionate sex, even during times of disagreement or even feeling somewhat disengaged from one another, it does not mean that your wife can. As many wives have come to understand the importance of being available for their husbands, it, of course, does not mean their needs or desires are exactly the same. The wife truly needs that emotional connection to more fully enjoy sexual intimacy with her husbands.

However, for the sake of the marriage relationship, wife's very often meet their husband's needs with the best attitude they can possibly have. Husbands should let their wives know how much they appreciate their effort in sharing this special gift with them. Also, many husbands need to understand that even when their wives are fully engaged and desire lovemaking with their husbands, they may or may not have a need to reach orgasm. Many times, a wife feels a deep contentment and bond with her husband just to fulfill him sexually and enjoy physical and emotional contact with him. Husbands who do not understand this sometimes get upset that their wives are not seeking the intense release they are.

Gentlemen you need to understand your wife is not wired the way you are emotionally or physically. She does not always need to respond sexually the same way that you do, and it is perfectly normal, and in no way does it mean that she is not engaged in sharing her love with you. You would be wise to stop making demands on your wife due to your lack of understanding concerning her emotional and physical makeup. Rather, I would encourage you to be grateful for her loving support and thank her for it rather than being frustrated she is not meeting some demand that you have placed on her.

As lovemaking is designed to be the giving and sharing of a gift to bless and enrich someone else's life we should develop an attitude of enjoyable expectations and expressions of deep love and intimacy.

As I have shared many of my thoughts and will continue to do so in the remaining pages of this book I thought it would be beneficial to also share the thoughts of several female authors on the topics of sexual intimacy.

In her book entitled, <u>Sex Let's Talk About It,</u> Wendy Treat shares the following." *Ladies, have you ever noticed there are times when your husband seems to get edgy? You may think he is mad or upset with you, but it's probably much deeper. Even though women can do almost anything a man can do regarding salaries and careers, they don't have the same makeup as a protector and provider that God instilled in men. Have you ever thought about how your husband feels the night before he makes a big presentation or a new job interview or promotion?*

He's probably nervous. Minister to him. Being a wife is a ministry. Be wise. Give yourself to your husband and assist him in actually flowing in the power of God. Doesn't that sound unique? It is amazing what your ministry to him can do. Sex is the most exciting experience a man can have in his life, and it is the most earthshaking, wonderful experience he can think of when it's with you."

Beverly LaHaye, in the book that she and her husband Tim wrote entitled <u>The Act of Marriage</u>, explains that "*a man's sex drive is physiological and a man can have sex multiple times a day, depending on his age. This is possible because the male body produces hormones constantly within his body that create a tremendous sex drive. This is not abnormal. He's not filled with the "lust of the flesh".*

<u>Intimate Issues</u> is a book written by two female authors, Linda Dillow, and Lorraine Pintus. In their

effort to help women understand God's plan for sexuality, they share the following.

God's voice declares: *I gave the gift of sex that you might create life.*

The gift of sex gives us the unspeakable privilege of creating a child from our love.

God's voice declares: *I gave the gift of sex for intimate oneness.*

Isn't this an incredible thought? Two separate beings become so bonded, so connected, so woven together in body, soul, and spirit that God sees them as being one rather than two. God's word says our sexual oneness is an earthly picture of the spiritual oneness Christ has for His church Ephesians 5:31 – 32

God's Voice Declares: *I gave the gift of sex for knowledge*

The Hebrew word for "sexual intercourse" is the word "to know." Through God's gift of sex, a husband and wife receive an intimate knowing of one another that they have with no one else.

God's voice declares: *I gave the gift of sex for pleasure*

Let your love and your sexual embrace with your wife intoxicate you continually with delight. Always enjoy the ecstasy of her love. Proverbs 5:15, 18 – 19 TLB

It would be difficult to find stronger words than intoxicate and ecstasy. These are God's words; this is his voice saying to you, "Enjoy your husband, give to him, and receive from him. Delight yourself in the erotic feelings of sexual love."

God's voice declares: *I gave the gift of sex as a defense against temptation*

To make certain His gift is used for good -to create a child, to give unique knowledge, intimate oneness, pleasure, and comfort, He wrapped His gift within the bonds of the marriage vows.

God's Voice Declares: *I gave the gift of sex for comfort*

While grieving, David comforted Bathsheba, his wife, and went into her and lay with her. So she bore a son, and he called his name Solomon. 2 Samuel: 12:24 Such lovemaking is rich with compassion and love... No wonder it brings solace!

The Song of Solomon is a book in the Bible that paints a picture of God's indescribable and unconditional love for his people while sharing the love story of King Solomon and his bride.

The graphic descriptions of sexual tension and sexual love are clearly stated. Their anticipation builds until they enter the bridal chamber. We are reminded in this writing that the Lord is the creator of all of our senses, sight, taste, touch, hearing, and smell. All of their senses were instrumental in their sexual union. To this young bride, there was no one as handsome and strong in her eyes as Solomon. From the physical strength of his body to his head of hair to his charming and flirtatious manner, all is described.

This may not be the same wording that you would use, but if you can imagine living in the days of Solomon, this would be one of the most beautiful and poetic terms of endearment a woman could imagine hearing. From the first of the story, Solomon states that Shulamith is the most beautiful woman of all the women in the kingdom. You are as exciting, my darling, as a mare among pharaohs stallions. Of all of the women, you are the one that would have all of the strongest and most handsome men stirred up and chasing after you. How lovely are your cheeks; your earrings set them afire! How lovely is your neck, enhanced by a string of jewels?

Her observation then continues by saying, the king is lying on his couch, enchanted by the fragrance of my perfume. My lover is like a sachet of myrrh lying between my breasts. It was customary in that day that a lady may have a small locket of blossoms creating a desirable fragrance on a chain between her breasts much as the perfume would be worn today. She's stating, my lover is laying on my chest as we love being close and holding one another.

The comments continue, you are so handsome, my love, pleasing beyond words! She simply did not have the words to express how handsome her husband was to her. She is so proud of his appearance and states, "If there were a great orchard, there would be no fruit-bearing tree as desirable as he is. "She literally found strength in his love. As he escorts her into the banquet hall, she states it is obvious how much he loves me. She literally says, "*I am weak with love*". An example of a lover absolutely being intoxicated with passionate love. Then she describes that his left arm was under her head, and his right arm embraced her. That is the description of a passionate moment between two lovers.

Let me see your face; let me hear your voice. Does that sound familiar? Was that the type of loving feelings that you had when you fell in love with your husband or wife? Is that the type of love you still share with one another?

And then the words of infatuation, "*You are beautiful, my darling, beautiful beyond words.*" He saw the beauty of her eyes, her hair, her teeth, her smile, her lips, her cheeks, her neck and her breasts are all described as beautiful and tender and desirable.

Chapter 4:9 reveals the depth of how lovesick they truly were. "*You have captured my heart, my treasure, my bride. You hold it hostage with one glance of your eyes, with a single jewel of your necklace. Your love delights me, my treasure, and my bride. Your love is better than wine, your perfume more fragrant than spices. Your lips are as sweet as nectar, my bride.*"

This section of the story continues as she is described as "his private garden, my treasure, my bride, a secluded spring, a hidden fountain. You're a shelter, a paradise with rare spices." He states you are my personal and private place of nourishment and refreshment. You are like an oasis that brings me comfort.

Then the young bride says, "Come *into your garden, my love; taste its finest fruits*". "Now, I have entered my garden, my treasure, my bride! Oh, lover and beloved, eat and drink! Yes, drink deeply of your love." And as only a sensual and lovesick bride could state,' *his mouth is sweetness itself; he is desirable in every way.*"

And then a declaration that states the beauty of their love,

"*I am my lovers, and my lover is mine*".

It is my prayer that those who read or hear the words of this book can come to understand the depth of God's love as well as the depth of his love that can flow through your heart into your husband and wife. May you grow in an understanding of spiritual, emotional, and physical intimacy for the remainder of your married life.

May you say to your husband and wife in sincerity, love, and with a lifelong commitment.

I am my lover's, and my lover is mine!

Contact Information:

Nathan Grooms Ministries

PO Box 99

Lincolnton, NC 28092 USA

nathangroomsministries.com

Facebook and Instagram

Nathan Grooms Ministries is a 501(c)(3) organization

www.ingramcontent.com/pod-product-compliance
Lightning Source LLC
LaVergne TN
LVHW051037070526
838201LV00010B/233